FIGHT FOR

The Life

YOU

WANT

A Dreamer's Guide To A

Happier Life

John Simmons, PhD

Published in the England by Stickman
Productions.

Scripture quotations are from THE NEW
KING JAMES VERSION.

Printed in Florida, USA.

ACKNOWLEDGEMENTS

I would like to express my gratitude to everyone who has helped and supported me throughout the process of writing this book. First and foremost, I am extremely thankful to my family for their unconditional love, encouragement, and belief in my abilities. Their constant support and understanding have been invaluable, and I could not have accomplished this without them.

I would like to express my sincere appreciation to my friends and colleagues who provided me with valuable insights and feedback. Your contributions have played a significant role in shaping this book and improving its overall quality. I am deeply indebted to my editor, whose expertise and guidance have been instrumental in refining and polishing the content. Your meticulousness and attention to detail have truly enhanced the final product. I would also like to acknowledge the reviewers and critics who took the time to offer constructive feedback. Your insights and suggestions have contributed to making this book a more comprehensive and thought-provoking read. Lastly, I want to express my heartfelt gratitude to all the readers who have supported and embraced my work. Your enthusiasm and passion for literature are what keep writers like me motivated to continue creating and sharing stories.

To all those mentioned above and countless others who have played a role in making this book possible, I extend my deepest thanks. Your contributions have made this journey an unforgettable one, and I am truly grateful for your presence in my life.

Thank you all.

John F. Simmons

CONTENTS

1

INTRODUCTION

"Until you make the unconscious conscious, it will direct your life and you will call it fate."

~C.G. Jung

I recall standing in the student allied health building with a panic attack as I contemplated how my life had become an unmitigated mess. The previous semester was undoubtedly the worst yet, and now here I am at another crossroads where crucial decisions must be made that could impact me for years to come. It's during these critical moments when we need clarity of thought and purpose if we want our choices to have lasting effects on both ourselves and those around us. As a pharmacy student at the time, I must admit that my presence in such an academic program was questionable. The reason for this lies within myself - lacking clarity about what direction or purpose would guide me through life made it easy to say yes when presented with becoming a pharmacist by family members.

Don't let anyone else hold the pen when crafting your life story. Take control and write it yourself. This is a chance to showcase who you are and what matters most in life. Embrace this opportunity with open arms! As a young adult pursuing higher education in pharmacy, I had high hopes for my future career prospects. However, despite being accepted into the program with ease - it quickly became apparent that this path was not meant to be mine.

My lack of interest and disconnection from professors made learning difficult; causing me to struggle through lectures without retaining much information at all. As time went on it became clear that becoming a pharmacist wasn't something that truly resonated with who I am as an individual. This realization hit hard when faced with failing two crucial classes needed for advancement within the program. In order to continue along this route would require sitting out for one year before retaking those courses again. Despite feeling discouraged by these setbacks, I know now that everything happens for a reason- perhaps there is another path waiting just around the corner?

As I waited for a chance to speak with someone from the student allied health department at my university... standing still wasn't easy. My mind raced through all sorts of life changing thoughts including joining military service - something that would have been unimaginable just months earlier! And yet here I was imagining myself being told "soldier shut your mouth" while trying desperately to make an argument. there's no denying it: I'm still figuring things out.

Though pharmacy may seem like an obvious choice given my academic background and interests in science, there is one thing holding me back: happiness. Despite having spent countless hours studying drug interactions and dosages over the years, I can honestly say that becoming a pharmacist doesn't excite or inspire me anymore. It simply isn't what makes me happy – which means it's not worth pursuing further.

As I waited patiently for what seemed like an eternity, a gentleman emerged from around the corner. Although his name and official title escape me nowadays, I am forever grateful that he took time out of his busy schedule to speak with me at length about my concerns. Have you ever noticed how sometimes talking through personal issues can be easier when discussing them with someone outside your inner circle? This is because strangers often offer fresh perspectives without any preconceived notions or judgments attached - making it easier to speak honestly and authentically.

INTRODUCTION

He listened attentively for approximately thirty minutes before abruptly interrupting me and stating that I had squandered enough time with my life already. It was essential to get focused on school immediately if there were any hopes of graduating successfully - according to him! Prior to this moment, neither education nor personal aspirations held much significance in my mind; henceforth everything changed drastically thanks to his intervention.

The words spoken by the gentleman had left me feeling shaken up and introspective. I couldn't help but reflect on my own shortcomings as a person who hadn't yet found their true calling in life. However, despite this setback, I refused to accept failure as an option for myself. Instead of wallowing in self-pity or denial, I decided to take action by scheduling a meeting with Dean Beck -the dean of student allied health... two days later.

Upon arriving at her office, Dean Beck's warmth made it feel like homecoming; she was kind hearted and compassionate towards me from the start. After spending some time together discussing various topics related to my future goals, she suggested that occupational therapy (OT) could be something worth exploring further. Although initially unfamiliar with what OT entailed, her confidence in me gave me hope that there might indeed be more out there waiting for discovery beyond just being labeled "unsuccessful". With renewed determination, I began taking steps towards gaining admission into the program through completing necessary coursework requirements.

As I completed my volunteer hours in various healthcare settings, a new perspective emerged. With each passing day, the image of myself as an OT became clearer and more vivid. It was like seeing everything through fresh eyes - including my own life. This experience gave me renewed hope for what lay ahead on this journey towards becoming an occupational therapist.

The OT program was my next target after applying for it. However, Mr. Walker who oversaw this department made his views clear about its futility - with over 300 applicants vying for only thirty-two spots available and given that I lacked competitive grades- he believed applying would be a waste of time. me included! Therefore, don't squander either our precious moments on something unproductive like this one again; let us focus instead on what matters most: achieving success through hard work and dedication towards our goals!

As they say "what GOD has planned for you will come to fruition no matter how long or difficult the journey may seem at first glance" so keep pushing forward until victory is achieved! As fate would have it, I was accepted into the program and appointed class president. With hard work and dedication, I completed all requirements with honors (thanks to Dean Beck). This achievement is something I'm proud of as it represents my commitment towards academic excellence. My academic struggles were largely due to my lack of intentionality when it came time for growth. I found myself comfortable with simply attending class day after day without any real focus or direction in life beyond that point.

However as anyone who has ever experienced this knows - comfort can be a dangerous thing! In order to truly expand one's mind and reach new heights requires effort- something which many people are hesitant about making if they're already content where they stand at present moment. But why settle for mediocrity? Why not challenge ourselves instead? That is what true success looks like: taking risks, stepping outside our comfort zones, and pushing past boundaries we never thought possible beforehand.

The idea that simply enrolling in school would guarantee success or even graduation is a fallacy. To achieve growth and attain the life I desired required effort - constant fighting against complacency was necessary if progress were to be made. Watching others play out their lives while remaining idle on my own sidelines wasn't an option anymore; it was time for me take action! With this new found determination came empowerment- I could finally see myself moving forward towards accomplishing what once seemed impossible before. And so began my journey into self-discovery, personal development, and ultimately achieving greatness beyond measure.

When I think of fighting for what I want in life two boxers come to mind - both battling it out inside a ring. The intensity required during each round is immense; with split second decisions being made constantly while punches are thrown back and forth between opponents who have trained their bodies beyond limits that most people can imagine! And when knocked down onto the floor after taking an unexpected hit? Do you stay there or do you get up again? It's all about resilience and determination: getting right back into action even if it's tough going at times because ultimately that's how we achieve success!

Life can be tough at times - we all face setbacks and challenges that knock us down. But it's important not to let these moments define who you are or limit your potential for growth in the future. Instead of giving up when things get hard, choose instead to rise above it by getting back on track towards achieving what matters most to you personally or professionally speaking. By doing so, you'll demonstrate resilience as well as an ability to forgive yourself (and others) while also fostering feelings such as pride joy & happiness within oneself over time through perseverance despite any obstacles encountered along the way!

As I reflect on my past experiences, it becomes evident that throughout much of my life I have been too like the boxer who decides not to rise after being knocked down. Instead of feeling discomfort from every step taken towards standing up again; comfort was what mattered most at those times in my life when things got tough or challenging. This mindset prevailed during many phases earlier on but has since changed as time passed by and wisdom gained through experience helped me understand better how important resilience is for growth both personally & professionally.

Today -I know-that staying still means stagnation while moving forward guarantees progress! So, no more giving into fears or doubts anymore because there's always something worth fighting for even if it's just one small victory each day!

The mindset that someone else will move us is problematic because we all must paddle our own canoe. If you sit back and rest instead of actively steering yourself towards your desired destination then by default you'll drift along with the flow - which only ever goes downhill! So don't wait for others; take control of where life takes you today.

John Maxwells words ring true when he says that everything worth having comes with an uphill climb. We may not always recognize this fact in our daily lives but upon reflection we can see its truth. When were comfortable and complacent about what we have achieved so far, we tend to focus on avoiding loss rather than pursuing new goals or aspirations. However, if only more people had clear objectives, they wanted to achieve then I believe they would be amazed by their own abilities once accomplished! The journey towards success is never easy but it's certainly rewarding - keep pushing forward no matter how steep the incline might seem at times!

It's a sobering thought that despite years of experience and knowledge gained from living life only 5% ever achieve financial independence. many people pass away within seven years after retiring; furthermore, most individuals are dissatisfied with their jobs while money-related arguments remain commonplace among couples or families alike. As children we had such vivid imaginations filled with dreams for our future lives - where did all this optimism go? Why is true happiness elusive for some folks when it should be something attainable by everyone? We must ask ourselves these questions if we want to live fulfilling lives free from regret.

In conclusion: Our journey through life can lead us down different paths but ultimately, it's up to everyone how they choose to navigate them. By staying positive about what lies ahead and taking proactive steps towards achieving personal goals one can increase the likelihood of experiencing genuine joy along the way. Remember: Happiness isn't just an emotion – it's also a choice!

Thucydides' words hold true for individuals just as much as they do nations or communities - "The secret to happiness is freedom, and the key to that lies in courage." How many people have you encountered who possess such bravery? And are these folks truly content with their lives? Similarly, Jesus Christ once said: "Straight is the gate but narrow its pathway; few find it though many seek after it." Could this suggest that achieving peacefulness may be challenging yet ultimately rewarding? Ultimately both quotes encourage us all towards personal growth through self-discovery while acknowledging how rare true fulfillment can be. worldwide.

The idea that happiness is an internal process rather than something derived from external factors was emphasized by one of my mentors. He explained how there exists almost complete correlation between levels of consciousness and feelings of contentment - those who are more aware tend to experience greater joy regardless of their circumstances while the unaware remain unhappy despite any gains they may have made externally speaking.

Earl Nightingale echoed this sentiment when he suggested that true happiness comes through progressively realizing a worthy goal or ideal; it cannot be achieved solely through material possessions or other outward markers of success. The beliefs we hold about life and happiness are crucial in shaping our experiences. To ensure that these convictions serve us well requires examining them closely for their realism, logic, and effectiveness. By taking responsibility for personal growth through facing challenges head on while staying focused on extracting maximum value from every experience can lead to fulfillment across all areas of ones being. This book aims at providing readers with an approachable formula which helps achieve this goal by unlocking the potential within themselves. May it bring you closer towards achieving your desired level of contentment!

Life is a journey that offers endless opportunities for growth and development. While we may already possess many skills necessary to navigate through life successfully, there's always room for improvement. By actively seeking out ways in which we can learn from our experiences rather than simply reacting passively - whether good or bad- we open ourselves up to new possibilities and perspectives on the world around us.

It's true that everyone has their own unique set of challenges they must face throughout their lives; however not all individuals take time reflect upon these obstacles objectively before moving forward. Instead, some people continue banging against imaginary walls without realizing how much control they have over their situation! Don't let this be you: instead focus on learning valuable lessons from each experience so that you can grow stronger with every passing day.

Remember that no matter what happens along your pathway through life- there are always chances available for personal advancement if only one chooses to seek them out proactively. So why wait? Start today by taking stock of where you currently stand while setting goals towards future progress!

Regardless of where you are in life or how things may seem at this moment, I want to extend a hand and assure you that there is so much more within than meets the eye. You possess an incredible capacity for growth beyond what could ever be imagined by most people - including yourself! Your potential knows no bounds; it's time to unleash it all!

ACTION EXERCISES

Imagine a world where success is guaranteed. What would you pursue? With no fear of failure what could be possible for your life? Take some time to reflect on this question and consider how it might shape the way you approach future endeavors.

If you were to depart from this world immediately would your actions and identity leave behind a sense of fulfillment? Take some time to reflect on whether you're satisfied with what you have accomplished thus far.

Take stock in who you are as an individual. If you were to leave the world right now, would you be content with what you've done here and who you've become?

Take some time to ponder this question and consider discussing it with someone close. Your answers could reveal important insights about what matters most in your life right now.

2

WHERE ARE YOU STUCK?

"Men are anxious to improve their circumstances, but are unwilling to improve themselves."

~James Allen

Life can be unpredictable at times - one moment everything seems fine and then suddenly something happens that throws us off course. This was the case for my friend who had an incredible opportunity to marry her college sweetheart after graduation. They were so in sync with each other during their time together as students; it seemed like they could anticipate what each would say before words left their mouths!

Their relationship continued blissfully post-graduation, but over time things began changing gradually yet significantly between them both personally & professionally. As they grew spiritually through faith practices while starting a family together, it became evident how much love remained within this couple despite any challenges faced along the way towards building lasting happiness together forevermore!

My friend was a true inspiration when it came to valuing family life. She spoke fondly of being both wife and mother, exuding an infectious energy that made everyone around her feel uplifted by their presence alone! Her creative prowess knew no bounds either - she had the ability to come up with groundbreaking ideas across various industries such as business ventures fashion or interior design without breaking sweat! It's safe to say that anyone who got acquainted with this remarkable individual would be left feeling inspired for years on end after meeting them once in their lifetime. just like me!

Her world was shattered when her husband approached her with the news that he no longer wished to remain in their marriage (only for him to remarry within six months of obtaining a divorce). This event left an indelible mark on both parties involved. My friend's journey through this life changing event was increasingly challenging as she struggled to come to terms with the fact that things would never be quite the same between her and her ex.

Suddenly transformed from a vivacious spirit into someone who had stumbled upon quicksand - stuck in place without any clear path forward- my friend's mindset around family left them feeling paralyzed at the thought of reentering dating after being together for over eleven years. As they navigated their way through these difficult times it became apparent just how much work lay ahead if they were ever going to find peace again.

WHERE ARE YOU STUCK?

Becoming stuck can have a profound impact on all aspects of your life including physical health mental clarity spiritual connection and emotional wellbeing. Without proper attention this experience will gradually drain away vital energy from within you, preventing you from reaching full potential as an individual. The inability to move forward hinders growth opportunities that would otherwise be available for personal development. Therefore, it is crucial not only acknowledge but also address these challenges head-on with determination and resilience.

We are meant to experience constant expansion across all aspects of our existence - physical, mental, and spiritual. If we fail at this task then it's guaranteed that things will only get worse! There is no such thing as stagnation; everything moves forward or backward without pause. a state of growth or decay defines every moment in life. Embrace change by seeking out opportunities for improvement daily.

Have you ever experienced an epiphany that changed your perspective on life? A moment where everything clicked into place and made sense in a way it never had before? These moments of clarity can be fleeting but they have the power to transform our lives if we act upon them. Too often though people find themselves stuck at crossroads unsure how move forward because they've become numb to their current situation. Therefore, it's so important not let ourselves get complacent or resigned when faced with challenges - doing so only leads us further away from fulfillment and happiness! Instead embrace change by taking action towards what truly matters most for YOU. Only then will you break free from stagnation and start living up to your full potential!

In 2007 I had an epiphany while driving to work listening to the "Frank Ski Morning Show" on V103. Frank included a segment called inspirational vitamin that provided listeners with spiritual guidance even if they didn't attend church regularly. He was gifted at combining music and thought-provoking messages filled with power into his broadcasts - something truly remarkable! The experience left me feeling inspired by both the content and delivery of Franks message which still resonates today. as it did then.

While commuting during peak hour traffic on this morning, I tuned into a segment featuring Pastor Craig Oliver (now Dr. Craig Oliver) who spoke about breaking free from holding patterns in life by introducing his message with the title "Breaking the Holding Pattern". As soon as those words caught my attention, I couldn't help but listen closely to what he had to say next. According to him we often find ourselves stuck between where were currently at and where we want/need be due to various reasons that may seem insurmountable - making progress towards our desired destination seems almost impossible! However, through faith & perseverance coupled with taking action steps towards achieving goals set out for us; we can break away from these limiting beliefs and move forward confidently towards fulfillment of purpose. ultimate success lies within reach if only one has courage enough to take hold of it!

Pastor Oliver used an analogy of a plane that had arrived at its destination but was unable to land due either logistical issues or heavy traffic congestion. The aircraft circled around the airport for upwards of thirty minutes before receiving clearance from Air Traffic Control (ATC) allowing it to descend and safely land. In essence, this situation represents what is known as "holding pattern" - dealing with delays during flight operations.

I was caught in a holding pattern without realizing it. My daily routine consisted of waking up, going to work, and hitting the gym before starting all over again tomorrow. I had become so comfortable with this cycle that it felt like listening to an endless song from a soundtrack - stuck on track one forever. Pastor Oliver's message touched upon many important points but what stood out for me were his statements about being willing to go down new paths: "You must be open minded enough not to rebel against change" he said; "Don't get trapped by repetitive ways of doing things- try something fresh instead"; and finally, "Your ability to reach your destiny is directly related to how responsive you are

towards visualizing your desired future."
Amen! These words resonated deeply within
me as they highlighted my need for personal
growth through adaptation and innovation.
The key takeaway? Embrace change if we want
progress.

The world around us is constantly evolving at
an unprecedented pace. In order to thrive in
such a dynamic environment, we must
embrace the importance of learning and
adaptability. We need to be able to
continuously learn new skills, reassess our
existing knowledge base and apply what we've
learned effectively. This requires flexibility and
resilience - qualities that are essential for
success in today's rapidly changing landscape.

One memorable example comes from a
speaker who opened his presentation by
bringing out a six-foot-tall dinosaur model
onto stage before writing "RTC" on the flip
chart with big letters. He then produced a live
white mouse from his briefcase and let it run
freely between his hands for about half a
minute. Looking up at the audience he asked
rhetorically: "Who would have betted against

this little guy surviving alongside giants like these sixty-five million years ago?" The message was clear: being resistant to change can limit one's potential for growth and progress. which ultimately leads to failure. The world we live in today is constantly evolving thanks to technological advancements. Social media has become an integral part of both our personal and professional lives. Research shows that businesses regardless of size rely heavily on social medias involvement for success. Therefore, its crucial for companies to utilize this platform effectively if they want to remain competitive.

To challenge myself I decided against using social media platforms for a prolonged period. At the time it seemed like too many people were wasting valuable resources on unproductive activities related to these sites instead of focusing on more meaningful pursuits. While some aspects of my reasoning held merit, ultimately, I realized that if I wanted to become someone influential or startup businesses successfully then adapting to modern trends would be necessary - including embracing digital technologies such as Facebook which is where I finally joined in 2016 during summer months. This decision marked a turning point towards greater success and fulfillment within both personal life goals and career aspirations alike.

Adaptation is crucial for survival in any environment. Our ability to assess and learn from our surroundings allows us to make necessary adjustments that lead towards optimal functioning within them. This process goes beyond mere change - it involves transformative shifts in how we approach life itself! As Tom Feltenstein rightly pointed out: "Change can be good... You go first!" But why do so many people struggle with this concept? The answer lies partly in human nature's resistance against alterations of any kind; however, embracing evolution as a way of being could help individuals overcome such obstacles while also ensuring sustained success over time. long-term growth becomes possible only through continual transformation – an idea worth considering if one wants to thrive amidst changing circumstances throughout their lifetime.

Don't let the postponement of your desired future become a distant memory because you remain STUCK. If pursuing objectives such as losing weight or quitting smoking is part of what drives you forward in life but results aren't forthcoming as quickly as hoped for don't allow frustration to take over and lead you down an unproductive pathway towards abandoning those goals altogether. Instead stay committed by taking stock of progress made so far while remaining open minded about alternative approaches that could yield better outcomes moving ahead. Remember: persistence pays off!

Life can be a tough journey filled with obstacles that threaten to derail our dreams. From discouragement and past mistakes to divorce or other challenges - there are many things that may cause us to lose sight of what we want most in life. But according to Joel Olsten these setbacks aren't meant to hold us back permanently; rather they serve as opportunities for growth if approached correctly. By embracing the difficulty instead of avoiding it we have an opportunity to develop resilience through adversity while also building character traits like perseverance and self-confidence along the way. As he put it so eloquently: "Remember that DIFFICULTY is not something to simply endure but rather an invitation to grow stronger." So, let's take up this challenge together by choosing courage over fear whenever faced with difficult circumstances!

ACTION EXERCISES

Where are you struggling in your life?

Which specific fears are preventing you from reaching your full potential?

Are there desires that you're not pursuing? Reflect on this question and consider whether there's something holding you back from going after what you want.

When was the last time you stepped out of your comfort zone?

Take the time to pen down your thoughts or ponder over them. Alternatively, engage in a conversation with someone close to you for deeper insights into these questions. This exercise will help broaden your perspective and provide new perspectives on life's challenges.

3

WHO IS GOING TO DO IT FOR YOU?

I am not what happened to me, I am what I chose to become

-C.G. Jung

My client recently underwent a drastic life change which resulted in losing several close friends. Their frustration stemmed from the lack of support they received when deciding to quit drinking and smoking - something that should have been celebrated by those closest to them as an act of strength towards living healthier. Instead, these "buddies" ostracized

him, leaving my client feeling alienated instead
of supported during this challenging time. As
their coach I empathized with how difficult it
must be for someone who is trying so hard at
making positive changes only to feel like they
are being judged or rejected because of it. My
advice was simple: surround yourself with
people who lift you up rather than bring you
down- it's never too late to make new
connections based on shared values!

My client was once at the forefront of his
social circle, leading frequent excursions to
strip clubs and bars with his friends. He had
ample resources that allowed him to cover all
expenses without hesitation - he simply
wanted everyone around him to have a good
time. His generosity made these outings even
more enjoyable for those who accompanied
him on their nights out. The realization that
his so-called friends were never truly loyal hit
home for my client. Once he stopped
providing them with liquor, drugs, and girls
they disappeared from his life completely -
leaving him feeling abandoned and alone.
Maya Angelou's words ring true here: "When
people show you who they are believe them

the first time." The truth is that many of us
have experienced similar situations where we
thought someone was our friend only to find
out later that they weren't as supportive or
caring as we had hoped. It can be tough but
ultimately, it's better to know upfront rather
than waste valuable energy trying to change
their behavior. In this case though it seems like
there may also have been other factors at play
such as financial struggles due to an
unfulfilling job which led him down a path of
risky activities in order to make ends meet.
Meeting someone special helped shift his
focus away from these negative influences
towards something more positive. Ultimately
however it takes courage to face reality head
on and move forward without relying on
others for validation or happiness.

To have any hope of marrying this young lady
and leading a normal life he needed to press
the reset button. When we embark on a
journey of self-improvement and growth it can
be disheartening to realize that some people in
our lives may not appreciate these changes. In
fact, they might even resent them! As
previously mentioned, no one truly enjoys

change - especially when it's forced upon us rather than chosen by ourselves.

The dynamics within any group or club rely heavily on consistency; everyone must adhere to certain norms for things run smoothly. When someone decides to deviate from this pattern through personal development efforts it upsets the balance- leaving others feeling uncomfortable with their newfound differences.

In conclusion: Change is never easy but sometimes necessary for progress; however, acceptance from those around you may prove challenging along the way. Don't let fear hold back your potential though – keep pushing forward towards becoming whoever you want to become despite what anyone else thinks about it! If you're part of a group that engages in negative activities such as smoking, excessive drinking or drug use on regular basis then changing your lifestyle can have an impact beyond just yourself. By choosing to distance yourself from these behaviors and opt for healthier choices instead you may be sending out signals that could make others question their own actions too. This might lead them to feel uncomfortable about continuing with their current way of life - which is why they may try to justify it by criticizing you personally! They may ask questions like "Who do you think you are?" or imply that somehow you believe yourself superior because of this change in behavior. However, remember that it's not always easy to break free from certain habits- so don't let anyone else define what kind of person you should be based solely on how different they perceive your newfound lifestyle choices to be compared to theirs. Instead focus on staying true to who YOU want to become while also being supportive towards those around you who may need help making similar changes themselves if desired. After all personal growth comes from within oneself first before anything else!

Change is often met with resistance because it challenges our comfort zones and forces us to confront uncomfortable truths about ourselves. This can lead people into justifying their thoughts, feelings or actions in order avoid feeling bad about themselves - even if they know deep down that what they're doing isn't healthy for them. But when you decide on making changes towards success- be prepared! It will require letting go of old habits & belief systems which may cause disruptions among those around you who are used to seeing things a certain way. By being aware ahead of time however; one can better navigate through these transitions without getting discouraged by unexpected reactions from others along the journey towards growth. Remember: change always brings forth new opportunities for personal development so embrace it wholeheartedly!

When we consider this matter carefully it becomes apparent that individuals who are dear to us as well as those whom we hold no strong feelings for may attempt unconsciously or consciously hinder our progress by keeping us in a state of stagnation. This is because they lack understanding about what we desire or fear change themselves.

In essence, when deciding on something new and different you must overcome the gravitational pull exerted upon you by everyone around due to their reluctance towards alterations taking place within them personally! Although it's possible to win over some people along your journey others will not accept the transformed version of yourself - but don't let this discourage you from moving forward with conviction! Remember: growth requires effort both individually and collectively; take charge of your destiny without expecting anyone else to do so on your behalf. keep pushing through any obstacles that come up along the way until success is achieved!

We often expect others to help us make changes in our lives but this approach rarely works out well. Instead of relying on external support we must take full responsibility for ourselves if we want progress. This means acknowledging that no one else can force change upon us or guarantee success - it all comes down to what actions we choose every day. As a young boy I remember feeling anxious whenever my teacher called on me during class time; specifically, when she asked someone to read aloud from the textbook.

My fears were realized each time as I struggled through words and stumbled over sounds while everyone watched silently. It was only after taking ownership of my learning difficulties by seeking extra tutoring sessions outside school hours did things start improving significantly. The lesson learned? Don't wait around hoping for assistance- instead focus on making your own way forward! The act of reading had become a daunting task for me as I struggled with identifying words on printed pages within books. After attempting to read through several sentences without success in recalling what was written down discouragement set in causing me to avoid any further attempts at engaging with literature altogether. Instead of focusing on studying diligently like most students would do; I honed my skills in charming teachers into believing that they were teaching their best student yet!

This approach worked well enough until one day when it didn't anymore- forcing me to confront the reality that there are better ways out there than relying solely on charm and good looks alone if you want academic successes worth celebrating over time.

My unconventional approach to education proved effective for twelve consecutive years until I finally graduated from high school. Despite one setback when my fourth-grade teacher attempted to persuade my parents into making me repeat the year (which thankfully did not happen due to Mom's intervention) -I persevered and emerged victorious with a diploma in hand! It goes without saying that this achievement was made possible by both hard work and dedication on my part as well as supportive family members who believed in me throughout it all. In the aftermath of my initial embarrassment about sharing this story with others during college years I've come to realize that there is power in vulnerability. By opening and discussing how difficult it was for me as a talented musician who struggled academically due to dyslexia - which affected reading comprehension- has allowed me to connect with people on an emotional level. giving them hope when they feel hopeless themselves. Through seeking help from professionals who diagnosed my learning disorder; I learned new techniques for approaching written material differently which ultimately led to academic successes beyond what anyone thought possible beforehand! This experience taught me valuable lessons about resilience perseverance & self-advocacy skills that continue serving me well today both personally professionally alike. It's never too late or impossible to overcome obstacles if we take action towards change instead of remaining stuck in shameful silence out fear of judgement from others around us. Remember: asking for support does not make you weak but rather shows strength because its takes courage to admit our limitations while still striving forward anyway despite setbacks along life's journey!

My personal story serves as a reminder that tackling barriers blocking academic achievements, professional growth or spiritual development requires proactive measures. By seeking help early on individuals can overcome obstacles and achieve their goals more easily than if they wait until things become overwhelming. Investing in oneself before asking others for support is crucial because it demonstrates commitment towards achieving success while also showing willingness to take responsibility for one's own life journey. This approach ensures greater chances of attaining desired outcomes without feeling like giving up too soon when faced with challenges along the way. Therefore, don't hesitate - fight for what you want most by acting today!

ACTION EXERCISES

In life we rely on certain individuals for support and guidance. Who are these people? Take a moment to reflect on this question as it may reveal some interesting insights about your relationships with others.

What are the things that you rely on them for?

Do you have significant things in your life that are being held up by others?

What actions would need to be taken for you to take the initiative and do what you've been waiting on others to accomplish?

To gain a deeper understanding of the answers, consider writing them out or discussing them with someone close to you.

4

WHAT IS IT YOU WANT, I MEAN REALLY?

"The person who makes a success of living is the one who sees his goal steadily and aims for it unswervingly. That is dedication."

~Cecil B. DeMille

Andy Stanley delivered a sermon that has stuck with me for years: "I am doing a great work and I cannot come down" Nehemiah 6:3. This message continues to inspire me today as it did then. It serves as an important reminder of the importance of staying focused on our goals even when faced with obstacles or distractions along the way. In this sermon, the speaker emphasized that one should not let DISTRACTIONS hinder them from accomplishing something positive. Don't allow yourself to come down off the wall and miss out on an opportunity for growth or impact. Stay focused! Nehemiah was entrusted with rebuilding the walls of Jerusalem. His adversaries had attempted various tactics to halt progress before realizing that everything depended on Nehemiah's presence in the valley of "Oh No." They invited him there for an assassination attempt.

Nehemiah's perseverance on the wall was crucial for his survival. Similarly, neglecting our own walls can have catastrophic consequences. We may not know what kind of impact we are making by staying focused and committed to doing great work- but it's important that we don't come down from it! Whether in family life or professional settings like churches schools or offices - each person has an opportunity to make a difference through their efforts towards building something meaningful. So, keep going strong knowing that your hard work matters immensely!

The potential for greatness lies within us all - but it can be easily thwarted by coming down from our high places. What obstacles are standing in your way? Are you allowing distractions or outside influences to derail progress towards achieving what matters most? Take stock of these challenges and consider strategies that will help keep focus on priorities while avoiding detours along the path ahead. Invest wisely in activities which align with goals rather than those which pull away from them; this approach will lead towards success instead of stagnation. Remember: it's never too late to start fresh!

When we have a clear objective that resonates with us on an emotional level everything else seems to fall into place. This includes decision making processes becoming streamlined while prioritizing tasks becomes second nature. Furthermore, distractions lose their power over our focus as they cannot compete against the motivation provided by pursuing something meaningful. So, what is it that drives you? What will ignite your passion and propel forward even before having consumed caffeine for breakfast?

The answer lies within discovering what truly matters most in life – because once found– success follows suit! The saying "No one washes a rental car!" is true because people don't feel the same way about something they don't own. Similarly, letting others dictate your goals can hinder progress towards achieving happiness in life. You deserve to pursue what matters most and attain success along with contentment as you work steadily towards fulfilling those aspirations. As Earl Nightingale said: "Happiness is the progressive realization of a worthy ideal." So, keep pushing forward!

The topic of desires is often overlooked by many individuals who tend to focus on what they don't want instead. Paul Martinelli notes that most people claim they desire a lot more than they do and settle for much less than could be easily obtained. This highlights the importance of being clear about one's aspirations in order achieve success. By defining specific goals one can work towards achieving them rather than simply wishing things would change without acting.

It's truly astounding when I come across individuals who desire a change in their lives but lack the motivation to fight for it. Believe me - we've all been through something that made us wish we could hit reset at some point or another! But acting requires stepping outside of our comfort zones; so instead many people choose to remain complacent with what they know rather than risking uncertainty and potential failure by trying new things. Therefore, it's important not only recognize opportunities for growth but also take proactive steps towards achieving them despite any initial fears or hesitations one may have. By doing this consistently over time you can create lasting positive changes within yourself as well as your environment.

As an occupational therapist I have had the privilege of working with many patients over time. One patient who stands out in my memory is Ms. Betty - a 48-year-old African

American female diagnosed with COPD, CHF, diabetes, HTN and chronic obesity while also requiring continuous oxygen at three liters per minute due to her difficulty breathing during activities like walking or standing for extended periods without assistance from a rolling walker. which she relies on for safe ambulation purposes. Despite these challenges however; Ms. Betty remains resilient and determined not let anything hold her back from living life fully! Her strength inspires me every day as we work together towards achieving our goals one step at a time.

She had a clear understanding of what she wanted to achieve - building up her cardiovascular endurance and strength so that managing self-care tasks at home would be easier. Additionally, resuming activities was also important for this individual who needed to reach an optimal level of fitness beforehand. Her determination towards achieving these goals is commendable!

Ms. Betty was aware of the importance of following a strict diet and exercise regimen in order to achieve her desired results. However, despite this knowledge she would often express frustration with these tasks upon my arrival at her home each day saying "I don't feel like doing anything." The smell of cigarette smoke lingered throughout Ms. Bettys room along with crumbs from potato chips and cookies scattered around her bedding; it became clear that she wasn't adhering to any recommendations we had made for improving her health status. which only worsened over time.

I asked her "What do you truly desire?" and she replied with honesty "I know that I require assistance because I cannot accomplish this alone." Take a moment to ponder what ignites your passion - those things which bring about an energy surge and purposefulness. the worthy goals and dreams are within reach if only we identify them clearly enough! Don't settle for anything less than fulfilling these desires; simply pinpoint their exact nature so they may become reality rather than mere fantasy.

The pursuit of a goal can be an invigorating experience that propels us forward in life. When we set our sights on something beyond what we currently know how to achieve it becomes necessary for us to take risks and tackle new challenges along the way - all while maintaining focus on where we want to go next. This process ultimately leads towards growth as individuals who can adapt quickly when faced with unexpected obstacles or opportunities alike. By staying committed despite any setbacks encountered during this journey one gains resilience and strengthens their ability to overcome adversity effectively over time. The rewards from such efforts include personal satisfaction derived from accomplishment as well as enhanced self-confidence resulting from pushing oneself outside comfort zones repeatedly until success is achieved at last!

So, if you're feeling stuck in your current situation consider setting some ambitious goals for yourself instead — they could very well lead down paths previously unexplored by you beforehand!

WHAT IS IT YOU WANT, I MEAN REALLY?

The pursuit of our desires can range from small everyday tasks to grand life goals that take years or even decades. These aspirations bring order into our lives by introducing structure and purpose. Without this sense of organization, we cannot achieve anything meaningful - there must be both movement towards something significant as well as a clear direction for where it leads us. James Allen's book As a Man Thinketh reminds readers about the importance of linking thoughts with intentions in order to create intelligent accomplishments. This concept highlights how crucial having clarity is when striving after what matters most in life.

When discussing the importance of having a clear objective in life many people quickly grasp that this leads to orderliness both within their thoughts and actions. However, when it comes down to identifying what exactly constitutes one's purpose or calling, they may struggle with finding answers. Peter Drucker offered some insight into this dilemma by stating "Only musicians, mathematicians and early maturing individuals have an idea about what they want from life at an early age." The rest must embark on a journey towards self-discovery through trial and error until they find clarity.

As you begin navigating your way along this path keep pushing past any obstacles which might hinder progress - for doing so will lead ultimately lead you closer towards fulfillment! Fear often tries to discourage us from pursuing our dreams by convincing us that they are unrealistic or beyond reach. It may suggest settling for what we already have rather than taking risks towards something greater. However, this line of thinking is flawed - it limits potential and stifles growth. Don't let fear hold you back! Instead aim high and embrace opportunities that come your way without hesitation. Only then can true success be achieved in life.

To overcome fears requires confronting them head on. Fear will always be present waiting for opportunities to discourage us from pursuing our goals or dreams during times of weakness. By removing the mask that hides its true nature we can see how absurd these worries are when viewed objectively.

WHAT IS IT YOU WANT, I MEAN REALLY?

Yes, falling is possible as well as looking foolish while making mistakes along the way; however, there's another side worth considering: getting back up after each setback and learning valuable lessons about resilience in life! With this mindset you'll have what it takes to achieve success despite any obstacles thrown your way. being willing to face fear directly is key if one wants to live a fulfilling existence without regrets later down the line.

By embracing mistakes you'll gain valuable insights and become an inspiration to those around you. This approach can lead to personal growth as well as positively impacting others' lives. Don't be afraid of making errors - they are opportunities for learning! I believe that the trials, mistakes, obstacles, and even temporary foolish moments are worth it. Why? Because they all contribute to something greater - a valuable lesson learned or an opportunity seized upon. To me this is what makes life meaningful and fulfilling.

ACTION EXERCISES

When was the last time you took a moment to reflect on your desires? Considering all that you want in life can be an enlightening experience. Take some time today and make this list for yourself - it may surprise you what comes up!

What are the five most significant objectives you hope to accomplish?

Which aspects of your life bring you true contentment?

What areas of your life are causing you discontentment? Identify these problematic regions and work towards improving them.

Pondering over the answers or discussing them with a loved one can help you gain new insights into your thoughts. Alternatively, writing out your responses is another effective method for exploring different perspectives and ideas. Whichever approach works best for you, make sure to take some time reflect on what's important in life!

5

WHAT IS REAL, THE DANGER OR THE FEAR?

"Our deepest fear is that we are powerful beyond measure. It is our light, not our darkness that most frightens us"

~Marianne Williamson

As a homecare therapist I am privileged to enter people's personal spaces - places where they feel secure and comfortable. This allows me insight into how individuals operate within their homes. It is an honor to witness this intimate side of life while providing care and support. As I stroll through their homes and engage with loved ones about family history, it becomes clear that these individuals once held significant roles both within the household as well as outside of it. Unfortunately, one issue which arises frequently is when patients fall in their own home but are unable to get up on their feet due to physical limitations - resulting in extended periods spent lying down (sometimes even days!). This situation can be quite problematic for all involved parties concerned.

When I assess individuals in their homes, my evaluation suggests that they possess the necessary motor skills to stand and walk. However, despite expressing a desire for mobility these people are unable to complete this task successfully due to fear of falling again. The more encouragement or motivation provided by me only serves as evidence of how overwhelmingly present this anxiety is within them.

WHAT IS REAL, THE DANGER OR THE FEAR?

This creates an unfortunate reality whereby those struggling with movement limitations perceive themselves as being physically limited when it comes down to standing up or taking steps without tripping - even though there may not necessarily be any danger involved at all! Fear has taken hold of their consciousness so much so that it becomes almost impossible for them to imagine doing anything else but stay still out of sheer terror.

The concept that we are born with only two fears is an intriguing idea which offers hope for anyone who has experienced trauma and struggles to live their life or achieve what they want. personal growth. As children develop through different stages, so do the fears they learn along the way. One such stage occurs around eight months old when babies begin understanding object permanence - meaning if something disappears it no longer exists. This leads into separation anxiety as seen in questions like "Where's Mommy?" or "When will she be back?". By recognizing these early developmental milestones, we can better understand how our own experiences shape us over time.

The development of imagination is a crucial stage in childhood that every parent should take note of. As their little ones grow older, they begin to create imaginary worlds and characters - including some who may not be so friendly! This can lead to fears based on things we cannot see such as the boogeyman lurking around at nighttime. One example from my own life occurred during a visit with family members down south when an intense storm hit our area unexpectedly. The thunder was deafening while lightning bolts illuminated everything outside like daylight; meanwhile inside mom's house furniture shook violently under each rumble of sound.

My mother screamed for us all to unplug electronics immediately before taking shelter beneath beds or couches until it passed by safely. Despite being young children themselves both nieces picked up on adult tension levels quickly thanks to parents' facial expressions alone! Through this experience I learned firsthand how important it is for caregivers to recognize these milestones in early childhood growth patterns so they can provide appropriate support throughout challenging times ahead.

As an aunt watching my nieces faces during this experience, I could see them struggling to grasp what was happening around us. They were learning from others fears rather than their own which would shape how they viewed similar situations in the future. However, it's important for parents and caregivers alike to remember that these stages of development are temporary - children can overcome challenges with time and effort! By encouraging resilience early on we help kids build confidence so when faced with scary moments later down life's road they know they have what it takes to handle whatever comes next.

As adults, irrational fear can be a barrier to achieving our goals if left unchecked. If this is the case for you then it may warrant attention and effort towards overcoming its influence on your life. By trusting in what we believe without question or investigation into alternative perspectives could lead us down paths that limit opportunities for growth personally or professionally speaking. The words of President Roosevelt during his inaugural address come to mind when he said "The only thing we have to fear is fear itself." These wise words remind us not to let fear hold us back from reaching our full potential as individuals capable of creating positive change within ourselves and beyond.

The fear we experience is an internal phenomenon that has no physical existence outside of ourselves. It manifests as a set of emotions, thoughts and behaviors which can sometimes even lead to bodily symptoms such as sweating or trembling. However, despite its subjective nature some may question whether it truly exists at all - especially when comparing two individuals who face similar circumstances yet only one feels afraid while the other remains unaffected by any sense of dread whatsoever. But regardless of how realistic this feeling seems for each individual person, there's no denying that fear plays a significant role in shaping our perceptions and actions throughout life. making it crucial for us all to understand more about where these feelings come from so we can learn better ways of coping with them effectively over time.

It's important to distinguish between fear and danger when discussing cars on busy roads. Yes - they can pose a significant threat if not approached with caution or respected as potentially lethal machines capable of causing harm at any moment in time! However, panic is only appropriate under certain circumstances where immediate action must be taken quickly before it becomes too late; otherwise sitting inside worrying about what might happen outside is an irrational response that doesn't serve anyone well over time because it's based solely upon imagined scenarios rather than reality itself. making it difficult for people affected by this type of anxiety disorder to lead normal lives without constant interruptions from their own thoughts

The idea that fear can be a helpful tool seems countcrintuitive at first glance. However, when we consider the fact that our bodies respond to both real and imagined threats in the same way - with an adrenaline rush and other physiological changes- it becomes clear why some people might rely on this emotion as a coping mechanism. The problem arises when we allow ourselves to become so reliant upon fear that it begins controlling us rather than serving us; avoidance behaviors may seem like effective ways of managing anxiety but they ultimately reinforce its power over us by preventing us from testing whether those fears are warranted. By acknowledging our concerns without giving them too much weight through rational thinking and practical precautions instead of emotional reactions alone we can break free from their grip and lead more fulfilling lives. Fear is just one aspect of human experience – don't let it define you!

Imagine yourself sitting in your living room lost deep within thought when suddenly an idea pops into existence - this one single notion can cause a ripple effect throughout every part of your body! The hormones released by the pancreas and enzymes produced by liver are all triggered by nothing more than what's happening inside our minds. cognitive processes have immense power over us- they determine how we feel physically as well as emotionally!

It's truly remarkable that something so seemingly insignificant like a mere thought could hold such sway over our biology; yet it does without fail each time we experience any form of emotional response! So next time you find yourself feeling happy or sad or angry for no apparent reason take note: it's likely due to some internal dialogue taking place unbeknownst even to ourselves!

Bruce Lipton's series on Conscious Parenting explores the impact of fear on our bodies and its effects on performance under stress. In his discussion he highlights three key things that occur when we experience fear: 1) Our cells shift from growth mode into protection mode; this means blood moves away from internal organs towards muscles in arms or legs to prepare for either fight or flight response against perceived threats. 2) The immune system shuts down since there is no point expending energy fighting off viruses which may kill us later if a lion could eat us now! These insights provide valuable information about how fear affects our physiology and can help individuals take steps towards managing their emotions more effectively during times of high-pressure situations.

The blood flow in our bodies is a fascinating topic that can help us understand how stress affects us. When we experience stress hormones are released which cause the blood to move away from the fore brain towards the hindbrain instead of being directed towards rational thinking processes like reasoning and logic; reflexive behaviors take over instead. This means that when faced with challenging situations where quick action is needed (like avoiding danger) we may not be able to think through things logically or rationally - leading us into troubled waters!

Furthermore, research has shown that most fearful thoughts never come true- making worry an exercise in futility since it doesn't lead anywhere productive. It's like chewing gum for your mind: it's something to do but ultimately produces no tangible results whatsoever.

In conclusion, understanding these physiological changes during times of stress could empower individuals by helping them make better decisions under pressure while also reducing unnecessary anxiety caused by unfounded worries. If loud noises or falling are keeping you from achieving your aspirations, know that they have always been present. Take comfort in this knowledge and keep pushing forward towards success. Remember that these fears don't define who you are as a person; instead focus on what drives you to achieve greatness despite them. With perseverance and determination anything is possible!

Our fears are often shaped by experiences we've had throughout our lives. These beliefs can cause us to feel doubtful or anxious when faced with certain situations - even if they aren't necessarily dangerous! But what many people don't realize is that these negative emotions are not set in stone; rather, they are learned behaviors that can be unlearned and relearned over time. through intentional effort.

If you find yourself feeling held back from pursuing your goals due to persistent feelings of anxiety or uncertainty, it's worth examining the underlying beliefs behind those emotions so that you can begin taking steps towards a more fulfilling life. With some work on mindset adjustment, anything is possible! Don't let fear hold you back any longer – start making progress today.

WHAT IS REAL, THE DANGER OR THE FEAR?

ACTION EXERCISES

What fears keep you up at night?

Fear is a natural emotion that we all experience at some point in our lives. But what are the specific things that give us pause?

Are any of these fears preventing you from reaching your desired goals?

Overcoming one or more of these fears could bring about significant changes in your life. What would those alterations look like for you?

To gain deeper insight into your thoughts and beliefs, consider writing out or discussing with a loved one the answers you come up with. This exercise can help clarify what matters most to you in life.

6

DOES EVERYONE SEE IT THAT WAY?

Men are disturbed not by the things that happen to them, but by the views they take of them.

~ Epictetus

As avid foodies who love trying out new places in town we were thrilled when a freshly opened restaurant received an enormous amount of media attention. Our group decided that this was something worth experiencing right away - hence our decision to make it happen soon! During dinner time we caught up on each other lives since last meeting while enjoying delicious meals from the menu at hand. However, as conversations flowed naturally between us all eventually talk turned towards Colin Kaepernick's highly publicized controversy within San Francisco's football team- The 49ers. We couldn't resist discussing such an intriguing topic among ourselves and debating different perspectives on what had happened so far with him being at center stage for many months now. It made for lively conversation indeed!

The United States was abuzz with talk about Colin Kaepernick's decision to refuse standing during the national anthem as a way of protesting against how African Americans and minorities were being treated by authorities. The issue he highlighted included police brutality towards these groups. In his own words, "I am not going to stand up for pride in a flag that oppresses black people." This sparked intense debate among friends at our table - usually we can agree on disagreeing when opinions differ but this time one person got emotional because they felt like Colins actions went beyond patriotism into unpatriotic territory. They couldn't accept someone disrespecting their country so openly without criticism or consequence.

As I worked through my imaginary chef's hat and put on my coaching one instead something clicked inside me. Suddenly all the pieces fell into place when recalling an empowerment exercise shared by Roddy Galbraith called One Hundred People Technique. This technique has proven to be incredibly effective in helping people achieve their goals. With this newfound knowledge at hand, I was eager to implement it immediately!

When I posed the question to my friend about imagining one hundred individuals who were experiencing similar emotions as him and asked if they would all respond in a manner identical to his own, he replied without hesitation that it was highly likely. He believed this because according to him there is only one appropriate way of dealing with such situations which everyone should follow - hence leading them towards uniformity when faced with comparable circumstances like these. His conviction left me impressed by how much thought had gone into his reasoning process behind arriving at such an opinion.

I responded by posing a question: "What other potential ways of reacting could there be?"

After some hesitation he acknowledged that there may be individuals who could potentially feel even more outraged and offended than himself.

I asked, "Are there any other names that caught your attention?"

Some individuals may not find this matter particularly bothersome. As one person put it "I guess some others might just shrug their shoulders."

I encouraged them to explore other responses by asking, "What else could you say?"

After a brief period of brainstorming, he emerged with an array of potential responses - anger, laughter, indifference, offensiveness, pleasure, scornfulness, sarcasm, and guiltiness. These were just some examples that could be used to convey different emotions or attitudes towards the situation at hand. With so many options available it was clear that there was no one size fits all approach when dealing with such situations.

I asked, "Do you truly believe that some individuals may react in these various ways?"

He had no doubt that they could achieve their goals.

I posed a question to my audience: "Is it possible for individuals to have varying reactions towards the same event? If so, can we conclude that it's not necessarily due to external factors but rather an internal process?" I concluded by emphasizing how crucial it is to recognize each person's unique experiences and perspectives. thereby promoting empathy and understanding in our interactions with others.

It was a pivotal moment for him as he finally acknowledged that his emotions were being triggered by something within himself. Moreover, the realization dawned on him only after performing the exercise - an experience which proved to be instrumental in achieving this breakthrough. This discovery highlights how crucial it is not just understanding concepts but also putting them into practice when seeking personal growth and development.

We are not troubled by the events of life itself. Instead, we find ourselves disturbed by other factors that impact our daily lives.

Our perception of events is shaped by the lens through which we view them. - Epictetus

When you grasp that your beliefs are the driving force behind how you feel about things in life it can be quite empowering. The truth is that it's not what happens to us but rather our interpretation of events through our lens of beliefs which dictates whether we experience joy or sadness for example. Similarly, perception plays a crucial role too - shaped by acquired knowledge and experiences over time- yet ultimately both stem from learned convictions formed during childhood years onwards. By understanding this relationship between emotional responses & belief systems one gains greater control over their own happiness levels! When faced with a situation that seems limited in scope some individuals may feel compelled to pursue only one course of action. This narrow viewpoint can lead them down an unproductive path as they repeatedly attempt the same approach without success - much like banging their head against a wall repeatedly! In contrast others see multiple options available for addressing this challenge; by exploring different choices these people avoid getting stuck in repetitive cycles that yield little progress or results.

The key takeaway here is: don't limit yourself when approaching difficult situations- explore all possible solutions before deciding on which one works best for you! Why do some individuals struggle with seeing the glass half full? Instead, they choose to focus on its emptiness. When things don't go as planned why is it so easy for us to say "I knew this was too good be true" or "Everyone seems against me"? These statements reveal a deep-seated belief that we are not worthy of success and happiness in life - which couldn't be further from reality! Let's challenge ourselves today by choosing gratitude over negativity when faced with setbacks or disappointments. allowing positivity into our lives instead of dwelling on what could have been. Our thoughts have a profound impact on our emotions and physical wellbeing. While we may not intentionally invite certain ideas into our minds it doesn't mean that they should control us. With mindfulness practice and self-reflection, we can learn to recognize these intrusive thoughts without allowing them to dominate our lives. "Colossians 3:2 urges us to prioritize our thoughts on heavenly matters rather than earthly ones."

In his book "A Better Way to Think" H. Norman Wright emphasizes the importance of kicking out unwanted guests from our minds as quickly as possible. He compares this process with physically removing intruders who enter your home without permission - it's essential that we act immediately rather than allowing them stay and cause harm or discomfort. The key lies in being aware enough about what's happening around us so that we can identify potential risks early on before they escalate into bigger problems later down the line. By having more options available at any given moment, we increase our chances of making informed decisions that align with our values and goals. Remember: awareness equal's power! In relationships, allowing oneself to repeatedly respond in the same way due to a belief that they are right can lead to perpetual disagreements. These conflicts may continue for years without resolution as individuals become entrenched within their respective positions. Even after one party has passed away people still harbor negative emotions such as anger or resentment towards them when thinking about past disputes. However, by seeking alternative ways of approaching situations rather than simply clinging onto what we believe is "right" could result in more positive outcomes and better communication between partners.

By adopting this mindset, it becomes possible to move beyond old patterns of behavior which have not been serving us well - leading instead towards healthier interactions with others over time. By being open-minded enough to consider other perspectives on issues at hand we allow ourselves room for growth while also fostering deeper connections with those around us.

In any relationship both parties have an obligation to work together towards mutual understanding and growth. However, if one person is struggling with seeing things differently than their partner who has greater awareness then it falls upon them to act in moving forward. This idea can be seen through the lens of a scene from Night at The Museum where Ben Stiller's character engages in repeated physical altercations with a monkey only for Teddy Roosevelt (played by Robin Williams) to intervene asking why he was hitting the animal instead of trying to understand its behavior better? Larry responds that "he started it" but Teddy retorts with a question about evolution: "Larry, who's evolved?" In essence - those with higher levels of consciousness must lead by example when navigating complex situations within relationships or else risk stagnancy.

T. D Jakes emphasized that the true battleground is not external factors such as haters, enemies, or liars but rather within our minds. He also pointed out how debt and financial struggles can be detrimental to one's mental health if left unchecked. It's crucial for individuals seeking success in life to focus on cultivating positive thoughts instead of dwelling on negative experiences. By doing so they will have a greater chance at achieving their goals while maintaining emotional stability along the way.

The Mind Is the Real Battleground

Don't let other people define who you are or what's important in life. Instead focus on your own thoughts and beliefs because they have the power to shape everything from relationships with others down to career successes over time.

Those around us may try to influence our decisions through their words but ultimately it comes down to how we interpret those messages ourselves - which is why it's crucial not just for happiness but also long-term achievement that we prioritize self-reflection above all else when crafting our narrative about ourselves. By doing so we can create a more fulfilling existence based solely upon personal values rather than external factors beyond control such as popular opinion or societal norms. So, take charge of your destiny today by focusing first within before looking outward at others' opinions!

Gaining a higher level of awareness is no easy feat - it requires more than just going through life's motions. To truly grow from our experiences, we must evaluate them critically and extract valuable insights that shape how we perceive reality itself. This process takes time but with intentional effort towards self-reflection over extended periods individuals can achieve greater levels of consciousness about themselves & their surroundings alike. So, if you want to improve your overall understanding of the world around you then focus on cultivating this mindset!

ACTION EXERCISES

What is preventing you from advancing towards your objective or aspiration? Identify the obstacles that are holding back progress and take actionable steps to overcome them.

Are there any other options available instead of not moving forward? Identify them.

Consider listing five different possibilities for action irrespective of their feasibility. This exercise in creativity could yield unexpected results!

Is there anyone you know who might approach this situation differently? If so, what would they do?

To gain deeper insight into your thoughts and beliefs, consider writing out or discussing with a loved one the answers to important questions.

7

ARE YOU MILKING THIS?

Every action has its pleasures and its price.

~ Socrates

Ms. Doll, an elderly lady I once spoke with shared a story about her grandson taking advantage of her unconditional love. She expressed disappointment in herself for allowing this to happen while carrying the weight of his past hurts on her shoulders. Ms. Dolls willingness to bear another person's burden highlights how much she cared about him and wanted what was best for him despite their relationship dynamic.

The words of an abusive mother who inscribed in her child's mind that he would never amount to anything set the course for his destructive life. This essentially stole away any hopes or dreams he had about become someone else entirely. The damage caused by these statements cannot be understated and will likely impact this individual's future significantly. Moving down south from Chicago to live with his grandmother was a decision that eventually led the young man towards an unforgettable experience of love and care. His grandma, Ms. Doll had only one goal in mind - showering her beloved grandson with all things genuine! She celebrated every milestone achieved by him be it academic or personal achievements while also being there as his biggest supporter for his dreams of becoming a singer/performer someday soon. The memories created during this time will remain cherished forever.

Unfortunately for her grandson, he struggled with addiction and found himself incarcerated on multiple occasions. Despite this setback however, his devoted grandmother never wavered from providing him with a haven upon release each time. She believed that she had an obligation to care for him due to the trauma he experienced during childhood; hence why she continued putting herself into debt by meeting all his needs and desires without questioning whether they were necessary expenses. Despite witnessing firsthand how little progress was being made over two decades worth of promises made by her grandchild - promising change but failing to deliver results consistently- she remained steadfastly optimistic about their potential future together as family members who could overcome any obstacle if only given enough patience and support.

Ms. Doll's grandson went to great lengths in order to feed his drug addiction by stealing from her home and misusing her credit cards without any remorse or guilt. This behavior ultimately caused a rift between them that has yet to be mended fully even after years of trying.

Their relationship was a one-way street where she gave while he took without any reciprocation. Her failing health forced her to confront the reality that change wasn't coming from him and she felt foolish for allowing herself to be blinded by love alone. She recalled an incident when she fell in her home but despite being just down the hallway away from her partner didn't come forward until after calling 911 emergency services arrived instead. This experience made it clear that his self-centeredness prevented him from showing empathy towards others needs or concerns - including hers! In hindsight this realization brought clarity on why their connection remained unbalanced throughout its duration.

There are two distinct types of individuals that exist in society - those who contribute positively to others' lives and those who drain them. The former group adds value by leaving people feeling better than they were before meeting up with them; while the latter tends

ARE YOU MILKING THIS?

towards selfishness at times taking away from
what could have been gained through
interaction. These contrasting approaches can
be seen when considering how different
people view situations from their own
perspective versus someone else's'. Ultimately,
it's important for us all to strive towards being
more like life giving individuals rather than
draining ones if we want our relationships with
others to flourish over time.

To seduce someone, we don't boast about
ourselves; instead, we focus on their strengths
and accomplishments. By highlighting what
makes them great we create an emotional
connection that can lead to lasting
relationships. This approach is not only
effective but also empowering for both parties
involved in the interaction. It's not uncommon
to hear about the lady who had dinner with
Mr. Gladstone one night and then dined with
Mr. Disraeli on another occasion - both
prominent English Statesmen of their time.

In her own words, "I believed Mr. Gladstone
was the most intelligent individual in all of
England after dining with him." However, she

later remarked that following a meal with Mr. Disraeli "I felt like I could hold my own against any intellectual challenge!" It seems both men were equally impressive in their respective ways! Life giving individuals have an uncanny ability to elevate both our mood and perspective on life. They leave us feeling uplifted not only about ourselves but also the world around us - infusing hope into every interaction we share with them. It's always a pleasure being in their company as they lift everything they touch!

Life draining individuals often have a self-centered outlook and focus on themselves when conversing with others. This can leave you feeling depleted after spending time in their company! It's important to recognize these types of people so that you can avoid them or limit your exposure if necessary for optimal mental health. Most individuals are unaware of their true motivations. A wealthy individual may claim that they work hard and earn money for the sake of supporting family members but, this is not always accurate. When spending time with loved ones it becomes apparent how little interaction there truly is between them due to feelings of anger or high expectations from said person towards others within their circle who feel unable to meet these standards set by someone else's definition of success. It seems like her actions are not aligned with what she claims to be doing for the family. Could there be underlying motives? She relishes in receiving attention and admiration from others while also enjoying not having any responsibilities towards raising children of their own.

While some people may enjoy the luxury of financial stability and a steady job other are forced into poverty due to unemployment. This can result in relying on state benefits for survival which often means enduring hardships such as limited funds for fancy cars or designer clothes or traveling abroad. However, is this really what we want? Is it truly convenient living with constant deprivation? The appearance of things can be deceiving - often what we see is not the whole truth. This holds true for those who are unemployed or retired; while they may seem to have all day free because they don't report into an office every day their lives could still be filled with responsibilities and obligations that require attention.

In order to progress towards a better future, we must learn how to let go of what holds us back. If you truly want mental and emotional wellness then it's crucial that you stop seeking pity or sympathy from others on an ongoing basis! Similarly, if creating strong family bonds is important for you then prioritizing quality time spent together should take precedence over other activities which may hinder this goal. And finally, when it comes down to landing your dream job - focus solely on improving yourself as much as possible rather than clinging onto any perceived benefits associated with being unemployed at present. By letting go of these things holding us back we can make room in our lives for positive change and growth.

The notion that there could be any positive aspect to experiencing misery may seem outrageous and offensive at first glance. But don't let this stop you from considering it further! Instead of immediately dismissing the idea or seeking validation elsewhere try exploring its potential benefits instead - who knows what insights might emerge? By taking an open-minded approach we can gain new perspectives on even challenging situations in life.

As per Paul Martinelli's teachings on the four pillars of drama people often seek out opportunities to feel offended. This tendency is something that we should all be aware of in order not fall into this trap ourselves or enable others who do so regularly. By being mindful about how we approach situations where someone may take offense, we can avoid unnecessary conflict and foster more positive relationships with those around us.

Why would anyone seek out offense? It's because they stand to gain something from it.

Socrates famously stated that self-knowledge is crucial for a fulfilling existence. In other words, the unexamined life lacks meaning or purpose. Are you willing to make sacrifices in order to gain deeper insight into who you are? Consider how convenient challenges may be holding back your progress and determine whether they're worth keeping around. With honesty comes clarity - so don't shy away from taking an honest look at yourself!

ACTION EXERCISES

Where are you struggling in your life?

Is there any silver lining to being stuck?

Are there any individuals in your circle who are experiencing difficulties with a particular aspect of their life despite possessing significant advantages from remaining stagnant?

To gain deeper insight into your thoughts and beliefs, consider writing out or discussing with a loved one the answers you come up with. This exercise can help clarify what matters most to you in life.

8

YOU ARE PERFECT JUST AS YOU ARE!

Be kind for everyone you meet is fighting a hard battle.
~ Socrates

Social media platforms have become breeding grounds for individuals who feel compelled to present themselves in a particular way. The pressure is on - if you want success or recognition online then it's imperative that your image aligns with what others deem as desirable. This often leads people down dangerous paths where they engage in body shaming behaviors towards those who don't fit into their idealized version of reality.

It's important not to fall prey to these unrealistic expectations and instead embrace the beauty within yourself just as it exists naturally without any need for alteration or modification. Remember- God doesn't make mistakes when creating human beings! Celebrate your unique qualities rather than trying to conform to someone else's idea of perfection.

I am deeply grateful to you for creating me with such intricate detail and beauty. Your handiwork is truly remarkable. My soul recognizes this truth wholeheartedly.
~Psalm 139:14

I was fortunate enough to attend the gospel competition "How Sweet the Sound" a few years ago where Donald Lawrence served as host. His words about embracing one's grace place resonated deeply with me because I have always believed that everyone has something valuable and unique, they can contribute to society. He emphasized how when we find our own personal grace place... things start flowing effortlessly; provision comes easily while doors open without resistance or obstacles in sight. This message left an indelible impression on my mindset which continues to inspire me today. It reinforces what I already knew - that each person's individuality is worth celebrating and should be cherished by all those around them.

In his opinion, operating within YOUR lane is the key to blessing others. God has bestowed upon everyone a unique set of gifts and graces that they can use for good in this world. However sometimes people spend too much time searching outside their area of expertise instead of focusing on what comes naturally to them - those things which are truly special because only they have been granted such abilities by divine providence alone! By embracing these talents we're able to make an impactful difference in our communities while also fulfilling our own purpose here on earth. making it possible for us all to thrive together as one united force for positive change!

Many individuals spend their lives pursuing careers that they excel at but lack passion for. However, when someone operates within the realm of what truly inspires them people are left in awe. The key lies in finding one's true calling and utilizing it to its fullest potential.

We all have unique abilities that make us stand out from others - whether its baking delectable pound cakes or cracking up everyone with your witty jokes. Jan is one such person who brightens up our weekly team meetings at work every Thursday morning by bringing in mouthwatering treats she prepared the night before! Her presence alone brings a smile to people's faces and lifts their moods instantly. Jan's baking prowess is truly remarkable. Her ability to create delicious treats that bring people together and make them forget about their diets is something special indeed! However, it seems like Jan herself may not be fully aware of her gift - she simply does what comes naturally for her. We are all grateful recipients of this wonderful talent. May it continue bringing joy into our lives!

YOU ARE PERFECT AS YOU ARE!

As children of God, we are all perfectly imperfect beings who must navigate through life's challenges with courage and determination. This sentiment was echoed by one of my mentors when they said "Having the bravery to say yes to existence is truly remarkable."

This statement resonates deeply within me because it highlights how everyday heroism can come from unexpected places - like a mother risking her own safety for another human being or a father standing up against injustice on behalf of his loved ones. community, or country. It reminds us that saying yes to our experiences no matter what they may entail takes immense strength-something worth celebrating!

We are all unique individuals with our own strengths and weaknesses. It's important to remember that not everyone can be a star quarterback or beauty pageant queen - nor should they have to! Instead, we need to embrace who we truly are and recognize the value in ourselves regardless of what others may think about us. success isn't always measured by external achievements but rather internal growth and self-acceptance.

Socrates believed that humans always choose good over evil because it aligns with their true nature as rational creatures capable of making informed decisions based on reasoned arguments. However sometimes this reasoning process might lead one astray if they lack sufficient knowledge or experience needed for sound judgment calls. Therefore, its essential that we approach life with an open mindset ready to learn from mistakes while also celebrating progress made along the way towards personal fulfillment. By doing so we cultivate resilience which helps us navigate through challenging times without losing sight of hope or purpose. understanding oneself better ultimately leads to greater happiness levels overall.

Throughout history countless wise individuals have emphasized the importance of knowledge by stating that ignorance is truly the only sin. one could commit in life. This statement highlights how essential it is for us to continually seek out new information and experiences so we can make informed decisions about our actions every day - leading towards a more fulfilling existence overall! Paul Martinelli echoes this sentiment when he suggests that "whatever lies ahead" should serve as your curriculum for personal growth; taking advantage of opportunities presented before you will help lead toward greater enlightenment over time. being open-minded enough to embrace change is key here too. So don't be afraid: keep learning, keep growing, keep exploring!

We often struggle with self-doubt and insecurity when comparing ourselves to others. but the truth is that no one person has an inherent advantage over another. Instead of focusing on what we lack or where we fall short, let's embrace our imperfections as part of who we are - because they make us unique! We can all strive for improvement by learning from mistakes and growing through experiences; this process leads not only towards better decision making but also a more fulfilling life overall. creating positive change within ourselves ultimately benefits everyone around us too. So why not choose forgiveness instead of judgment? Let go of grudges against those who have wronged you while seeking forgiveness yourself – after all its what Jesus taught us: "Forgive us our trespasses as we forgive those who trespass against us." Remember: together we rise above individual differences and create something truly remarkable!

Anthropologists who study African tribes often encounter unique customs and lifestyles that differ from their own. One such anthropologist spent considerable time observing the behavior of a particular tribe's children during his research. To engage with them on an interactive level he decided to play games one day - buying candy was key since they loved it so much! He arranged many pieces in a decorative basket atop which sat the prize: placed strategically near a tree base for added challenge.

With great enthusiasm the anthropologist gathered all children together and explained that they would be playing a game wherein only one winner could take home an entire basket of candy. The rules were simple: when he shouted "now" everyone had to sprint towards the designated tree as fast as possible - whoever arrived first won everything!

The kids lined up eagerly, each holding hands with their friends or siblings for moral support before taking off at full speed upon hearing those two magic words from their leader. As soon as they reached the destination simultaneously, they split up what was rightfully theirs without any hesitation or selfishness involved; just pure joy in sharing something special among themselves. When asked why they chose this approach instead of trying individually for personal gain alone- which many adults might do under similar circumstances- some replied simply because it felt like more fun that way while others shared how much better it made them feel knowing they'd helped make someone else happy too through such acts of kindness & generosity. This act of unity demonstrated by these youngsters left quite an impression on our observer who couldn't help but marvel at its simplicity yet profound impact on human relationships overall.

The Ubuntu philosophy emphasizes the importance of recognizing our interconnectedness as humans. Our actions have consequences that extend beyond ourselves - every decision we make either adds value to another person's life or takes it away from them. This means that even when we choose not do anything at all, we are still making a choice with far reaching implications for others around us.

By being mindful about this reality and taking responsibility for how we affect those around us through our choices each day; whether big or small- can help create positive change in society overall. We must always consider what kind of impact we're leaving behind on people after interacting with them because its crucial aspect of living consciously.

The concept of leaving behind a legacy for future generations is often associated with financial assets or inheritance. However, what about our daily contributions? Our everyday actions such as writing emails, sending texts, and making eye contact all contribute towards

YOU ARE PERFECT AS YOU ARE!

creating an enduring memorial that speaks volumes about who we are as individuals.

When viewed through this lens it becomes clear how important each decision can be in shaping the way others perceive us over time - so why not make them count!

ACTION EXERCISES

What aspects of yourself do you find unsatisfying?

How do they impact your existence?

To gain insight into your thoughts and beliefs, consider writing out or discussing the answers with a loved one. This exercise can help you clarify what matters most to you in life. Don't be afraid to take some time for self-reflection as it may lead to profound realizations about yourself that were previously unknown.

9

LOVE ALL LIFE, INCLUDING YOURSELF!

There are two basic motivating forces; fear and love. When we are afraid, we pull back from life. When we love, we open to all that life has to offer with passion, excitement, and acceptance. We need to learn to love ourselves first, in all our glory and imperfections. If we cannot love ourselves, we cannot fully open our ability to love others or our potential to create.

~ John Lennon

The people we encounter every day can be unpredictable - even those who seem friendly and approachable. In my condo building I rarely run into any of my neighbors outside of brief elevator conversations or chance encounters in the hallway. These interactions are usually short lived but they do provide a glimpse into their personalities beyond just what meets the eye. Despite this limited interaction with them on an individual level; collectively as residents within our shared space there is still much to learn about each other through these fleeting moments together. As such it remains important for us all to maintain openness towards one another regardless of how well acquainted we may already be!

While working out at the fitness center one day I struck up a conversation with my neighbor who shared their life story. As we talked more deeply it became apparent that they had faced significant challenges during childhood which still impacted them as an adult today. They revealed how low self-esteem and abandonment issues were causing frequent negative thoughts leading to occasional suicidal ideation along with sleepless nights. This was heartbreaking for me hear about someone going through such struggles alone without any support system in place. It made me realize just how important mental health is when dealing with trauma from our past experiences or current situations.

From then onwards I have been actively involved in helping others like him by providing emotional support whenever needed while also advocating for better resources towards addressing these types of problems within society itself.

I hope this inspires you too! You're probably thinking that he needs professional help. And indeed, at various points in time he has sought out such assistance and even taken medication to manage his illness intermittently. Yet despite these efforts towards self-improvement, he still views himself as undeserving of happiness - which often leads him down a path wherein he sabotages relationships just when they start getting serious. This pattern continues without any sign of change or progress being made on this front. It remains unclear whether more extensive therapy or alternative treatments could offer some relief for someone who seems so stuck in their own mindset.

It's heartbreaking to witness someone struggling with such intense emotions like unhappiness and depression. My friend has been vocal about his feelings but unfortunately seems stuck in a cycle of self-criticism where he constantly focuses on what he perceives as flaws rather than celebrating any positive developments happening around him. He dismisses anything good that comes along by saying it's just temporary or fleeting - which is truly unfortunate because there are so many things worth being grateful for! It's time we all take some steps towards cultivating more positivity in our lives instead of dwelling too much on negativity. I've learned that we all experience different seasons in our lives which is why I try not to psychoanalyze or pass judgment on others. Instead, my approach involves highlighting the good and successes of individuals. This strategy has proven effective while working with patients over time. It allows me to focus on what matters most - their strengths rather than weaknesses. By doing so, it helps build trust between us as well as encouragement for them towards personal growth.

It's important to remember that none of us are perfect. We're all going to mess up at some point or another because that's just how life works for humans. So instead of dwelling on our flaws and mistakes lets focus on learning from them so we can grow as individuals.

Surprising, isn't it?

The reality is that despite knowing full well about the inevitability of mistakes, detours, and unexpected outcomes along our journey towards success we often let fear hold us back from moving forward. Some people get stuck for days or weeks while others allow their dreams to be derailed permanently due to an overwhelming sense of failure.

But why? Why do we get stuck in certain situations?

Napoleon Hill reveals in the concluding chapters of Think and Grow Rich that there are six fundamental fears which hinder us from achieving freedom and success. These include:

The fear of poverty is a common concern for many individuals.

The fear of criticism can be overwhelming.

The fear of ill health can be overwhelming.

The fear of losing someone is a common experience that can be overwhelming.

The fear of aging is a common concern for many people.

The fear of death is a common phobia that many people struggle with.

These fears are fundamental. They stem from what we've been taught or experienced in life. Depending on the severity of these experiences our level of anxiety may vary significantly.

How do we combat fear? How can we overcome the irrational and negative thought patterns that trigger survival mode and limit our hope for a better future? These are important questions to consider as they have significant implications on how we approach life's challenges.

How can we lead a struggle free existence?

The encouraging news is that you can retrain your brain. Regardless of whether you're young or old negative thoughts are not permanent and can be identified, rejected, and replaced. With effort and determination anyone can transform their thinking patterns for a more positive outlook on life.

To gain insight into how this is achieved let's take a closer look:

The rewritten text should be no longer than twenty-four words and no shorter than eight.

Fear is intertwined with our perspective. It relates to how we perceive things and particularly ourselves. We tend to view situations through a personal lens or based on preconceived notions without much thought involved. This automatic process shapes the way in which we interpret events around us.

During dinner six or seven individuals engaged in a conversation about real estate investing.

As we delved deeper into the conversation, you became increasingly disengaged and checked out.

As an individual who is not involved in investing it's important to recognize that this activity may not be for you.

It's interesting to note that neither you nor your parents have ever owned a home. This means there's no experience with real estate investments either.

Instead of aligning yourself with something (which would be called leaning in) you may have chosen to distance yourself from it. This decision was likely made without any conscious thought or consideration.

The left side of our brain plays a crucial role in processing information from past experiences and relating it to current situations. This allows us to anticipate probable outcomes based on what we know so far. If you're surrounded by people discussing investment opportunities but don't believe they apply to your situation then it's likely that the left hemisphere has assumed about not needing this knowledge - leading you towards disengaging instead of staying engaged with the conversation at hand.

Hold on tight!

The idea that investing could impact your future success is worth considering. And if you're someone who didn't hit their stride until later in life but now recognizes the importance of owning property - this awareness can be empowering. With it comes the ability to learn, grow and make changes towards achieving what matters most for you personally. So don't underestimate how valuable having such insight into oneself truly is!

Napoleon Hill identified core fears that can hinder our progress towards achieving success. These fears rob us of power and limit our potential for growth. However, by embracing courage over cowardice we can overcome these obstacles and move forward with confidence in pursuit of what truly matters most to us.

Rather than permitting these fears to wreak havoc in our minds like an untamed banshee we must take control and

• Identify them

• Reject them and

• Replace Them

We are responsible for managing our own thoughts and beliefs by identifying negative ones that may be holding us back from achieving success or happiness. giving them the boot is crucial in order to move forward with confidence. However simply trying not think about something doesn't work - just try picturing a purple zebra right now! Instead, we need to adopt different strategies such as replacing old thought patterns with new positive ones through affirmations or visualization exercises.

By taking control of what goes on inside your head you can create lasting change in all areas of life including relationships career growth personal development and more. So why wait?

LOVE ALL LIFE INCLUDING YOURSELF!

Start today by kicking out those limiting belief systems once and for all! Instead of trying to suppress negative thoughts and fears we should focus on replacing them with positive ones. This involves reminding ourselves who we are what were made of and all that is available for us in life.

Affirmations can be used as a tool but only if you truly believe their message; otherwise, they won't work effectively. By adopting this approach towards positivity one can create lasting change within themselves over time. So why not give it try? The benefits could far outweigh any initial discomfort or skepticism! The Bible is a treasure trove of wisdom and guidance for believers. their daily lives are enriched by the simple yet profound scriptures that offer encouragement during difficult times. Consider these verses as your personal promises: James 1:2 states "Consider it all joy my brethren when you encounter various trials." Similarly, Peter writes in his first letter chapter one verse sixteen saying "In this situation rejoice greatly because although now temporarily distressing various trials have come upon you." Philippians fourteen verse

FIGHT FOR THE LIFE YOU WANT

thirteen offers assurance through Christ's strength with its message "I can do everything through him who gives me power." Finally, Hebrews thirteen twenty-one proclaims "You are fully equipped and limitlessly resourced to handle whatever comes your way today."

These words provide hope and comfort during challenging circumstances helping us persevere until we reach our desired outcome. giving thanks along the way! The Word promises us that we can always rely on God's grace to provide everything we need for every good deed. We are assured of this through 2 Corinthians 9:8 which states "And God is able to make all grace abound to you." This means that no matter what challenges or obstacles come our way, we have access to an abundance of resources and support from above. enables us stay focused on the path ahead without being distracted by fearful thoughts. As Isaiah 30:21 reminds us, when we listen carefully for guidance from God's voice behind us instead of giving in to lies from within ourselves or others around us - we become vessels filled with hope! By living out these truths daily we elevate ourselves into a higher vibrational frequency where positive results flow naturally towards us effortlessly.

Walking free from fear is a habit that can be formed with practice. It requires embracing who we are and living an authentic life full of courageous actions without hesitation or reservation. Remember failure isn't final - it simply means you tried something new! So why not give it your all? Whether successful or unsuccessful at least you were actively engaged in creating change rather than standing still on the sidelines watching others live their lives fully.

So go ahead- act today! Start small if necessary but start nonetheless because every step towards freedom matters greatly over time.

And always remember: "The only way to do great work is to love what you do." - Steve Jobs

Sara Blakely's journey to becoming the youngest self-made billionaire at age 41 is truly inspiring. Her success story as founder and creator of Spanx - a popular women's apparel product - has left many in awe but what really caught my attention was her father's approach towards failure when she was growing up. his philosophy revolved around embracing mistakes rather than fearing them which helped shape Sara into who she is today. Every evening he would ask "so, what did you fail at today?" if there were no setbacks or missteps Dad wouldn't be satisfied with their conversation over dinner- something that taught Sara resilience from an early age. making it easier for her later in life when faced with challenges while building her empire! This unique parental guidance proves how important it is not only to encourage children to take risks but also teach them how valuable learning through trial & error can be- leading them down paths they may never have considered otherwise!

To avoid stagnation in personal growth and development it is essential to step outside of one's comfort zone. This means embracing failure as an opportunity for learning rather than a setback. By doing so one can expand their horizons and challenge themselves towards greater achievements.

LOVE ALL LIFE INCLUDING YOURSELF!

By embracing failure as a freeing exercise in the process of becoming Sara was able to recognize that not experiencing any failures meant she wasn't pushing herself far enough out of her comfort zone. This realization allowed for growth and development beyond what would have been possible otherwise. By taking risks and being willing to make mistakes along the way one can truly achieve greatness.

Embracing life's mess is a daily challenge that requires us to be fearless and intentional about growth. When we strive for more than what was yesterday - when we chase after it without hesitation or reservation - only then can we begin uncovering our true potential as individuals capable of achieving great things! So, let's embrace the chaos with open hearts today; tomorrow holds endless possibilities if we do so bravely!

Life presents us with numerous opportunities to take risks and push past perceived limitations. Don't let fear hold you back! Embrace the chance to swim in deep waters or free fall without worrying about failure - because it happens sometimes but it's not final! You can always get up again try harder and eventually achieve success. Take control of your destiny by fighting for what matters most to you; don't settle until you have everything that makes life worth living!

ACTION EXERCISES

Are there any fears that are preventing you from living intentionally?

How do these emotions affect your overall well-being?

To replace fears with positive declarations in your life, what actions can you take today?

To gain insight into your thoughts and beliefs, consider writing out or discussing the answers with a loved one. This exercise can help you develop new perspectives on life's challenges while strengthening relationships along the way.

10

IF IT'S WORTH HAVING IT'S HARD TO GET!

I can sum up the success of my life in seven words. Never give up. Never, never give up.

~ Winston Churchill

For teenager's high school life is a crucial period where they form bonds with like-minded individuals who share their outlook on existence at that time. From football games to prom nights - this phase of life leaves an indelible mark on one's memories forever.

The devastation caused by Hurricane Katrina in New Orleans, Louisiana forced many people to flee their homes and communities. Among them was a young girl named Karen who moved with her family to Orlando Florida where they stayed with her grandmother. However, the move brought about significant challenges for everyone involved - including financial hardships as well as emotional turmoil due to displacement from familiar surroundings. Despite these obstacles though- through resilience & determination- Karen managed to navigate this difficult period of transition successfully. This story highlights how even during times of crisis or upheaval there is always hope if we remain steadfast in our resolve!

Karen's family faced significant challenges after moving to Florida - her mother struggled with unemployment while caring for them became too much of a financial burden on their grandmother who lived off fixed income. The result was that they ended up in shelters.

Despite these setbacks Karen remained resilient and continued attending school every day with an infectious smile on her face and pleasant demeanor. Even though she had limited resources like studying by candlelight at night due to poor living conditions, she refused to let it affect her academic pursuits negatively. I believe most people would have empathized with the difficult circumstances that led to this life-altering change for Karen but instead of feeling sorry for themselves or giving up hope altogether; she chose positivity and determination as coping mechanisms which ultimately helped her overcome adversity successfully.

Karen's journey towards academic success began with her graduation from high school as valedictorian. Her achievements continued into college where she received a full scholarship and graduated with honors in chemical engineering at the master's level. The spark of inspiration is an essential part of any successful endeavor - it marks when we give ourselves permission to pursue our dreams or goals wholeheartedly. This moment often comes accompanied by feelings such as determination, optimism, passion, and motivation that propel us forward on this path towards fulfillment. May you find your own spark soon! The beginning of something new is often exhilarating - full of promise and potential. It's like starting fresh with a blank canvas or entering an exciting relationship where everything feels possible. However just as in romance relationships the substance isn't built during this initial phase but rather through overcoming challenges together daily that shape who we are inside outwardly.

This process ultimately determines whether our dreams come true or fall by the wayside one choice at a time because it creates us from within outwards up until we become fully formed individuals capable of achieving great things. So, embrace these moments when you start something new knowing they will lead to growth and transformation if approached with intention and dedication towards building yourself up day after day!

Success is not something that happens overnight - it takes consistent effort and dedication every single day. Take a moment to reflect on your life as it stands now: what are you proud of? What have you settled for? And most importantly, what do you want to change? All these things can be traced back to the choices you've made up until this point in time. creating an environment around yourself that either supports or hinders growth towards success.

The art of living out one's passion lies within understanding how fluid everything truly is; constantly adapting while remaining steadfast throughout any challenges encountered along the way. This requires perseverance above all else! Remember: "Rome wasn't built in one day" so keep pushing forward with intentionality and purpose. If you're dissatisfied with your current situation, its time to start making choices that align with what truly fulfills and satisfies you. This requires a certain level of humility - an acknowledgement that where we are now is not necessarily where we want or need to be in order to achieve our goals. We must take responsibility for ourselves if we hope to grow into the best version possible.

IF IT'S WORTH HAVING IT'S HARD TO GET!

Excuses like "I was raised this way" or "I can't help it because that's all I know" won't get us anywhere good; they only hold us back from reaching our full potential. Its up to each one of us individually whether we choose comfort over growth or vice versa – but remember: living life on purpose takes effort! It may require stepping outside of our comfort zone at times but ultimately leads towards greater happiness and satisfaction. So why wait? Start saying yes today by taking ownership of who you are right now while simultaneously working towards becoming someone even better tomorrow.

Taking ownership of your past mistakes and failures is one of the most liberating experiences you can have. By standing on top of all that has gone wrong in life - broken promises, unfulfilled commitments, lies told or masks worn - and acknowledging it as part of who you are today; you create a starting point for change. This act requires vulnerability but also provides immense power over one's own future by saying "yes" to responsibility. It's like jumping out of an airplane with no parachute-both exhilaratingly risky yet necessary if we want anything different from our lives than what we currently have.

We can shape ourselves into whoever we want every single day. Each moment presents us with an opportunity for growth and transformation; there is no need to wait until Sunday or even tomorrow morning before making positive changes in our lives.

The power lies within each of us - all it takes is realizing when we're acting out of alignment with what brings joy and fulfillment into our existence, followed by taking immediate action towards correcting this behavior pattern through conscious decision-making processes that can be executed on demand at any given time throughout one's daily routine's schedule. The present offers limitless possibilities for personal development without restrictions imposed upon its timing or frequency! Start now if you haven't already begun your journey towards self-improvement!

The decision to adjust your alignment can be made at any time without delay. This act allows for permission once again towards fulfilling one's dreams, goals, and purpose in life. But how do these small choices affect my level of success?

To answer this question: The correlation between making tiny decisions and achieving significant accomplishments is noteworthy. By acting consistently over time - even if it seems insignificant initially- one gains momentum towards reaching their desired outcome while maintaining stability along the way. With each choice comes an opportunity for growth that ultimately leads us closer towards our goal. So don't underestimate what seemingly minor actions could mean for you!

The title of champion is not earned solely in the ring but rather acknowledged there. The true champions are those who put forth consistent effort and dedication towards their goals outside of competition.

Success is not just a destination but rather an indication of how disciplined and committed one has been throughout their journey. Just like physical muscles are proof that someone works out regularly; success serves as evidence for one's commitment towards achieving something significant in life.

Star athletes may receive recognition on the field after winning championships but they become champions long before stepping onto it by saying yes to pursuing their dreams every day through early morning workouts or rigorous training routines while others settle for mediocrity instead. The key lies within our daily habits - if we cheat there then failure will eventually catch up with us down the line. Ultimately true victory comes from within ourselves first before being recognized externally later.

Former heavyweight champion Joe Frazier once said "You can map out a fight plan but when the action starts it boils down to reflexes." This statement is not only true for boxing matches but also applies to every aspect of our lives. It highlights that success requires more than just having an idea or making plans - it's about taking consistent actions towards achieving your goals even if no one else sees them.

Frazier continued by saying "If you've cheated on roadwork in darkness then you will get found out under bright lights." This emphasizes how important preparation and discipline are when pursuing something valuable such as personal growth or career advancement. It's crucial to operate with integrity and make choices that align with one's aspirations rather than settling for mediocrity. Ultimately this approach leads to fulfillment and achievement. Therefore, we must remember that anything worthwhile comes at a cost- hard work!

Living with intention and fulfilling one's destiny is no easy feat - it comes at a cost. Choosing this path means facing obstacles head on; challenges that may test your resolve time after time. It requires immense self-discipline, unwavering commitment to the cause & constant reminders of why you started in first place when things get tough along the way! It's not always going be smooth sailing either- loneliness could set in as well as feelings of isolation from those who don't understand what drives us forward towards our goals. However, despite all these hurdles we must keep pushing through them because ultimately, it's worth it! So yes- choosing such an approach will require effort but if done rightly can lead one down path they never imagined possible beforehand.

If you choose to slack off or become complacent by settling for less than what's possible with your abilities, life will be tough. You'll constantly ponder about the possibilities that could have emerged had only changed some habits and pursued dreams wholeheartedly instead of staying within comfort zones. This lackluster approach may result in regrets later when looking back at missed opportunities; ones which would have brought immense joy through successes achieved outside usual boundaries. By not giving yourself permission to take risks earlier on, you might find it hard one day imagining how much more fulfillment could have been gained from an unconventional path taken instead!

When faced with two difficult decisions, it can be tough to determine which one is best suited for us. However, by considering both options carefully we may come across some important distinctions between them: One choice promises a fulfilling life and liberation while the other brings disappointment or regret into our lives instead. Considering this information my advice would be simple yet profound - choose your hard wisely! Remember that ultimately, it's up to you what kind of challenges you take on in life; just make sure they align with who you are as an individual so that success comes naturally from within rather than being forced upon yourself through external pressures alone.

ACTION EXERCISES

When we give up on something, how do we justify it to ourselves?

Do we acknowledge legitimate reasons for our decision?

What are the benefits of giving up in these areas?

What are the potential drawbacks of giving up in these areas?

Pondering over the answers or discussing them with a loved one can help you gain deeper insights into your thoughts. Alternatively, writing out your responses is

IF IT'S WORTH HAVING IT'S HARD TO GET!

another effective method for processing
information and developing new ideas.

11

FORGIVE FOR GOODNESS SAKES

"To forgive is to set a prisoner free and discover that the prisoner was you"

~Lewis B. Smedes

I have a story that may not be classified as funny per se but I believe it will make you chuckle nonetheless. Allow me to share with you this amusing anecdote and let's see what we think after reading through it together!

Dr. David Cooper, a revered pastor at Mount Paran Church in Atlanta Georgia penned down an intriguing story in his book "Preaching Through the Year." It revolves around an elderly preacher who summoned both his lawyer and IRS agent from among his congregation before passing away. him motioned for them to sit on either side of his bedside while holding their hands tightly. He then stared blankly upwards without saying anything until finally asked by the attorney why he had called upon them during such trying times. The minister replied with utmost humility that Jesus died between two thieves which is how he wanted to go too. This poignant tale highlights the importance of having faith even when facing death.

The story I just shared was meant to be humorous but unfortunately there is some truth behind it. Many people hold onto grudges and refuse forgiveness which can lead them down a path of bitterness that ultimately harms themselves as well as those around them.

When couples with children separate without practicing forgiveness, they create an environment where everyone loses out in the end. Similarly, siblings who cannot let go of past conflicts due to their unwillingness to forgive each other suffer from prolonged anger issues that negatively impact both parties involved. In conclusion holding on tightly to grudges only leads towards more pain rather than resolution or healing. Therefore, its essential for individuals seeking happiness and fulfillment to prioritize forgiving others instead of dwelling on negative emotions like resentment or hatred.

Forgiveness is often a difficult concept for families to grasp. But why? This article explores the reasons behind this challenge and offers insights into how individuals can work towards building stronger relationships through forgiveness. The Bible states that everyone has sinned and failed to meet Gods expectations. This is a universal truth that applies equally across all cultures, races, or social classes. It reminds us of our human frailty and the need for forgiveness from above.

WHERE IS MY WHY?

When we embark on the journey towards forgiveness it is common to encounter moments where those who have wronged us come into our thoughts. This can trigger feelings of discomfort or even physical reactions such as cringing when considering them again. It's okay though - being honest with ourselves about these experiences while reading this book will help us move forward in a healthy way. Don't be afraid to acknowledge what you feel!

The individual who sprung to mind just now serves as your personal symbol for unforgiveness. This person makes it challenging to contemplate the idea of starting anew with a clean slate. While you may be able to forgive many individuals in general, this figure remains difficult to pardon.

What's the Big Deal?

Life is full of ups and downs. People may disappoint us or cause harm along the way but we often carry these experiences with us as resentments, hurts, or anger towards them.

Left unchecked this can lead to bitterness or contempt for others over time. However, by focusing on love instead of negativity one can find empowerment in their daily lives rather than being held back by grudges against those who have wronged them previously. The key takeaway here is that there are two paths available - either choosing love which brings blessings into one's life or opting out of it resulting in bondage instead. This choice cannot be made without acknowledging its impact on our overall wellbeing both physically & mentally. So why not choose happiness? Start today by letting go of any negative emotions holding you back from living your best possible life!

There is no compromise when it comes to freedom versus bondage. You either embrace liberty or remain shackled by resentment towards someone who has wronged you in the past. It's essential not to make any exceptions for this individual as forgiveness remains key to achieving true liberation from their hold over your emotions and mindset.

But why? Why is it so detrimental to hold grudges against those who truly deserve them? After all there are some individuals out there who have committed atrocious acts. Is forgiveness simply about letting these people off the hook without any consequences or payment required for their actions? Does this mean that they can continue doing whatever they want with impunity? These questions may arise when considering whether holding onto resentment serves us well in life's journey towards happiness and fulfillment. while it may seem like an easy answer initially - it's not always as straightforward as we might think.

Forgiving someone doesn't necessarily equate with condoning what they did; rather it involves acknowledging our own pain and releasing ourselves from the emotional chains of bitterness and anger which ultimately only harm us more than anyone else involved. being able to let go allows us space to heal fully and move forward positively into a brighter future filled with hope and possibility instead of remaining stuck in cycles of negativity where no one wins. including ourselves! So next time you find yourself struggling with unforgiveness ask yourself: What am I gaining by holding on tightly to my hurt feelings? And could choosing differently lead me down a pathway toward greater peace within myself and relationships around me? The answers may surprise you...

To truly understand the concept of "payment" we need to examine it closely. When someone harms us do they pay for their actions? Or is it up to us to bear that burden instead?

Dr. Steven Standiford, chief of surgery at the Cancer Treatment Centers of America has revealed that unforgiveness is now recognized as a medical condition in various textbooks on medicine. This classification highlights its potential negative impact on individuals' health and wellbeing. It emphasizes how important it is for people to let go of grudges or resentments they may be holding onto. By doing so they can improve their overall physical and mental state.

Bottom line? Refusing to forgive will cause you harm and keep it that way.

In his book on forgiveness Dr. Michael Barry's research revealed that over 60% of cancer patients struggle with forgiving others and half have severe issues in this area. The impact is significant as it highlights the importance of addressing these challenges for those facing serious illnesses like cancer. This underscores how essential self-care practices such as forgiveness can be when dealing with chronic health conditions.

Unforgiveness can have a profound impact on our physical health by disrupting the natural order of things. When we harbor negative emotions like unforgiveness or hatred for extended periods they create chronic anxiety within us which then leads to excess production of adrenaline and cortisol hormones that inhibit vital cancer fighting cells from forming properly. This ultimately weakens our immune system making it more susceptible towards illnesses such as cancer. Therefore, its crucial for individuals who are struggling with forgiving others to seek professional help immediately before their condition worsens further.

Medical research has uncovered that unforgiveness can disrupt almost every bodily process. The impact of this is significant and far reaching making it crucial to prioritize forgiveness for optimal health outcomes.

It's important to note that not all sick individuals harbor anger, bitterness, or resentments. However, what I can say with certainty is this: holding onto grudges will have a detrimental impact on both physical health and mental wellbeing - hindering focus, peacefulness & productivity in life. Forgiveness offers freedom from these negative emotions while promoting overall well-being instead!

We often believe that by refusing to forgive someone we are inflicting punishment upon them. However, this belief is misguided - it's ourselves who end up paying the price for holding onto grudges and resentment towards others.

The act of withholding forgiveness may seem like a formidable tool at first glance but ultimately, it's an obstacle preventing us from moving forward in life; keeping us trapped within negative emotions such as anger or bitterness instead of allowing room for growth through self-reflection and healing processes. This article serves as a reminder that if you have ever thought "I will never forgive him/her" then now is the time to release yourself from these chains so that true freedom can be achieved!

The Greek word for forgiveness has a profound meaning - it translates into "letting go" or "releasing." This means that when we choose to extend forgiveness towards others, we are essentially throwing off any negative energy associated with holding onto grudges. It is an empowering act of self-care! By choosing not to harbor resentment and instead embracing the freedom that comes from letting go, we can cultivate greater peace within ourselves as well as in our relationships with those around us. So why hold on? Why not release what no longer serves you today?

In forgiveness therapy, it is reported that people experienced a physical sensation of lightness after they forgave someone. This suggests an incredible connection between our emotional wellbeing and our overall health. Consider how holding onto grudges or resentments can impact both your mental clarity as well as your body's ability to function at its best level.

The Bible provides additional understanding in Hebrews 12:15 where it states "See to it that no one misses out on the grace of God and avoid any roots of bitterness springing up which could cause trouble and defile many." This verse highlights how important it is for us not only receive but also apply this wisdom from Scripture. as we navigate life's challenges. By doing so, we can stay grounded in our faith while experiencing true freedom through Christ Jesus.

The concept of forgiveness is often discussed in religious circles to cultivate positive emotions such as love and joy. However, when we harbor grudges or resentments towards others - which can manifest into bitterness- it becomes difficult for us to produce good fruit that aligns with these virtues mentioned earlier. The Bible tells us clearly what kind of fruits are pleasing before God: those associated with the

Holy Spirit like peace, patience, gentleness etc.
So, if you want your life filled up with
positivity instead of negativity then it's time to
let go off any unforgiving thoughts or attitudes
towards anyone who has wronged you in some
way. It's not worth holding onto something so
destructive! Instead focus on nurturing healthy
relationships by practicing forgiveness
regularly.

Forgiveness - How Do I Begin?

Many individuals speak about the importance
of forgiveness. They cite research that
demonstrates its necessity and yet few possess
an understanding on how to practice it
effectively.

Forgiveness is a complex concept that can be
approached in various ways. Some people may
feel obligated to forgive others while others
might try praying or conjuring up feelings of
empathy towards those who have wronged
them. However, these methods are not always
feasible especially when dealing with
individuals who lack mental stability or
emotional maturity. Therefore, it's important
for us to recognize the limitations involved

and choose an approach that works best given our circumstances.

Forgiveness is a straightforward process that requires simplicity. Avoid complicating matters by involving the other party or waiting for an apology; this will only prolong your bitterness and prevent healing from taking place. Remember: forgiving someone does not require them to repent - it's about letting go of any grudges we may hold against others so that we can move forward with our lives without being held back by resentment.

The act of forgiveness involves casting off negative emotions towards another person while also setting ourselves free from their influence over us. It allows us to live in peace rather than dwelling on past wrongdoings committed against us. So why wait? Start today by practicing forgiveness and experiencing its transformative power!

To achieve genuine forgiveness, one must follow these steps:

Acknowledging that something unpleasant occurred is crucial for moving forward in life.

The first step towards healing involves acknowledging the reality of what happened without denying it or minimizing its impact on you personally. This internal agreement allows us to accept our experiences and begin processing them effectively. It's not about denial - rather an honest recognition that yes, this did happen- but now we can move past it with greater understanding and resilience.

Unforgiveness can feel like a burden that weighs us down - but it doesn't have to be! By making the decision to let go of grudges and resentments towards others or ourselves we release our minds from negative thoughts. allowing for new opportunities in life. Saying out loud "I release this person" is an important step towards moving forward without carrying around heavy emotional baggage. Remember: forgiving someone does not mean reconciling with them if you previously had a relationship- it's simply about letting go of negativity associated with past events so they no longer hold power over your present state of mind.

The opportunity to indulge in old movie replays may arise once again but it is up to you as the "bouncer at your minds door" to swiftly decline participation. Instead opt for filling your mind with more meaningful and positive thoughts by saying things like "God bless this person's life." This practice can help shift focus away from malicious intent towards understanding that everyone has their own core pain and damaged emotions which contribute to hurtful actions. By being proactive about ending cycles of negativity through acts such as sending positive energy instead of engaging in retaliation or revenge seeking behaviors, we become agents of change who promote healing rather than perpetuating harm.

By practicing these forgiveness steps you'll come to realize that every offense presents itself as an opportunity in disguise. When someone hurts us and we respond with blessing instead of retaliation or resentment - there is nothing more powerful than this act of love. By embracing such a mindset towards others through the practice of forgiveness one can find themselves empowered in all aspects of life; from speech to action- everything becomes infused with positivity when

approached with kindness rather than anger or
hostility.

ACTION EXERCISES

Who remains unforgiven in your life?

What are some things that you have not been able to forgive about yourself?

Have you noticed how the pain or guilt associated with this issue has affected different areas of your existence?

12

WHERE IS MY WHY?

The two most important days of your life are the day you were born, and the day you find out why.

~ Mark Twain

Every individual has a unique purpose in life that sets them apart from others. This internal version of yourself is equipped with distinctive gifts, talents and passions waiting to be unleashed upon the world. However, this true self can either remain suppressed or nurtured for growth through intentional effort on your part. The choice ultimately lies within you alone - choose wisely!

You are not replaceable by anyone else because no one else possesses exactly what makes up who YOU truly are as an individual; hence why it's crucial to embrace these differences rather than ignore them. allowing them to flourish into something meaningful instead of being stifled underneath layers of conformity. So go ahead-be bold enough to let your authentic self-shine brightly without apology or hesitation!

As adults we tend to overcomplicate things - including finding our 'why.' Children start out with a sense of wonder and optimism that knows no bounds. They say things like "I want to fly" or "touch the stars." But as they grow older limitations are learned through experience. As parents its crucial for us to nurture our children's dreams by encouraging them to explore their natural talents without fear of failure. success is not guaranteed but allowing children space to try new experiences can lead to lifelong benefits according to numerous studies on early childhood development.

The Bible also offers insight into this way of thinking: Proverbs 18:16 states that "A man's gifts will make room for him." This verse reminds us that pursuing what comes naturally can open doors in life that may have otherwise remained closed. So why complicate matters? Embrace simplicity and let your passions guide you towards fulfillment!

Your gift is a divine spark that sets you apart from others. It's the unique something inside of you that defines who you are and what purpose God has for your life. Your gifts connect to both passion and fulfillment; they're all part of finding out why we exist in this world. When we operate within our calling, even challenges don't seem as daunting because it feels like we were made specifically for such moments! Money or education aren't obstacles when pursuing one's destiny since it's what brings joy into one's existence. Says German philosopher Friedrich Nietzsche "He who possesses a reason to live can endure almost any how."

When it comes to achieving success in life many people believe that having a strong education is the key. However, as we can see from statistics on career fulfillment rates across various industries and educational levels - this isn't necessarily true. In fact, over 60% of workers report feeling disengaged or unfulfilled by their work despite being highly educated individuals with impressive resumes under their belts! This begs us to ask ourselves an important question: could it be possible that these professionals simply aren't pursuing careers aligned with what truly motivates them? Could they instead be stuck doing jobs that may serve others well but fail to inspire passion within themselves personally? If so, then perhaps it's time for each one of us individually to take stock of our own lives and consider whether we are living out our purpose fully-or if there might still be room left for growth and exploration towards greater meaningfulness in all aspects of existence including professional endeavors. spiritual practices etc. By focusing first on finding your "why" before worrying about how long or difficult something will be- you'll find yourself more energized than ever before when tackling new challenges along the way!

When we suppress our desire for personal growth and settle instead on paths that seem more secure or practical than what we truly want out of life, we are essentially denying ourselves the chance to live up to our full potential. This can result in feelings of dissatisfaction even if one has attained a high level of education - something will always feel "off" without pursuing one's individual purpose with passionate intentionality. Many people struggle with identifying this unsettling feeling but it's important not to ignore it; rather seek ways towards fulfillment through active engagement with your true calling!

The good news is that your 'why' remains intact and can be accessed at any time. Your internal compass still works perfectly fine, leading you towards the place where all your dreams are alive. The question now becomes: "Where did I leave my why behind? How do I find it?"

By making a conscious decision to give yourself permission to discover and live out your life purpose - even if only in theory right now - everything starts falling into place for you. This one choice marks the beginning of an incredible journey from darkness into light as the universe conspires with you every step along the way. From here onwards follow up actions will reveal themselves naturally so long as you remain committed to disengaging from others' expectations and tapping back into that inner child who once had big dreams.

And remember- it's never too late! So, start today by taking action towards finding what truly fulfills you in this world.

Do you recall the last time that woke up feeling truly fulfilled by your purpose or have you been consumed by deadlines and distractions from external factors? Consider how these influences may be impacting your overall sense of satisfaction in life. As we discussed earlier, being the bouncer of your own brain requires more than just focusing on positive thoughts and believing in yourself. You must also agree to protect the vision and purpose that has been given to you - even if it hasn't fully revealed itself yet. This commitment is crucial for achieving success and fulfilling one's potential. Remember: greatness awaits those who are willing to take risks and fight for what they believe in!

Living out one's purpose is not an easy feat; it requires constant effort and dedication towards nurturing dreams that align with this goal. This means making choices every step of the way - deciding whether to pursue opportunities presented along the pathway towards fulfillment. The key lies in recognizing these moments as they arise, taking action accordingly while remaining mindful about potential pitfalls such as fear or uncertainty which could hinder progress if left unchecked.

For those who may struggle with accessing their internal compass for guidance on how best approach these situations effectively it's important to note that there are ways around this challenge. Rather than being paralyzed by anxiety over what might happen should things go awry instead focus on developing a growth mindset where mistakes become learning experiences rather than setbacks. By doing so one can cultivate resilience necessary when faced with obstacles enroute towards achieving personal goals aligned with ones calling.

Don't let uncertainty hold you back from pursuing your purpose. It's okay not to have all the answers upfront - in fact its normal! The key is choosing daily to embrace opportunities that align with what drives and inspires you most without limiting yourself along the way. Remember: saying yes opens doors while setting limits closes them off prematurely. So go forth confidently knowing that every step taken towards fulfillment brings you closer than ever before!

When we choose to say yes and give ourselves permission to break free from self-imposed limitations our goals become clearer than ever before. The fact that you want them is all it takes for these aspirations to manifest themselves in reality; the more frequently you affirm your commitment towards achieving what matters most, the greater clarity will emerge

over time. You've only been stuck because
at some point along this journey you traded
away something valuable - purpose itself!
By exchanging dreams & ambitions for
seemingly easier or safer options we lost
sight of why they matter so much in first
place. But now it's up us regain control by
saying "yes" once again- giving ourselves
license to pursue passions without
reservation while trusting that everything
else falls into place as a result!

Living a life that fulfills your purpose
requires compromise.

It's inevitable and something you should
get used to early on. However, as time goes
by the voices of those things which once
seemed reasonable will start sounding
ridiculous. Take for example an
entrepreneur who started out cutting his
neighbor's lawn but now has seven crews
responsible for maintaining all golf course
properties within their town. over ten years
later. If someone were to offer him a

secure management job with hourly pay rate, would he take it? Absolutely not! His passion is already attached to his business; its where he's found fulfillment and growth opportunities alike. He's even provided jobs last month for two young men from the community reentry program who served jail time - giving them another chance at life. The point being: if living intentionally towards one's purpose means making sacrifices along the way then so be it- because ultimately, they lead us closer towards what truly matters most.

This entrepreneur's decision to pursue his lawn service company has led him down a path that he never could have predicted. The extra layer of fulfillment that comes with this venture connects him even more deeply with what drives him - changing lives for the better. When faced with an inner pull towards starting something new did he know how much well it would do? No, but he had enough courage and conviction to say yes anyway. And now

WHERE IS MY WHY?

look at where he's ended up! This is proof positive that following your heart can lead you places beyond imagination.

The question of where your inner compass is pointing you can be daunting. But by giving yourself permission to live out your greatest purpose and listening closely for guidance from within - you'll find what you seek because it already exists inside of you. So why wait? Start living the life that was meant for you today!

ACTION EXERCISES

Do you have any idea why your existence is significant?

Are you content with not understanding why you exist?

Do you have acquaintances who fervently pursue their purpose?

What impact does it have on their existence?

To gain deeper insight into your thoughts and beliefs, consider writing out or discussing with a loved one the answers you come up with. This exercise can help bring clarity to complex ideas while also fostering meaningful connections with those closest to us.

13

SUMMARY

God doesn't require us to succeed; He only requires that you try.

~ Mother Teresa

If you've made it this far through the book, I hope that my words have inspired within you a desire to fight for what matters most in life. Whether young or old there is no reason why anyone should ever feel limited by their age when pursuing goals, they believe are worthwhile endeavors. From today forward live with purpose and intentionality as each day unfolds before you; imagine yourself thriving at work after finally applying for that job opportunity which seemed too daunting previously while also envisioning successes related to starting up your own business venture or shedding those extra pounds once thought impossible! Don't let fear hold back progress any longer – act now towards achieving all that you truly want out of life.

A wise minister once stated that "you have to see it before you can actually see it."

This means that if we want others to perceive us as being or doing something different than what they currently do, then first and foremost we must cast a vision of ourselves in this new light. We need not only visualize these images but also make them vivid with bright colors and intricate details. The John Maxwell consultant tool called "The history of your future" is an

WHERE IS MY WHY?

excellent resource for helping clients quickly envision their desired future ten years from the present day - everything they ever wanted achieved! It's crucial though that while imagining such possibilities without judgment allows one to freely dream big; it's equally important never giving up on those aspirations despite facing roadblocks dead ends or unexpected obstacles along the way. Fighting hard for one's desired life is essential. So, keep believing in yourself and striving towards making those visions become reality! Discovery, ease, and pain relief are not guaranteed in life. Instead of relying on external factors to improve your situation take ownership over it yourself.

This may seem daunting at first but ultimately empowers you with the ability to start anew whenever desired. Don't wait for others - seize control now! Your life may be plagued by darkness and disappointment but hope springs forth from the shadows. The fear of failure can be overwhelming but it's important to remember that disappointment is temporary if you keep pushing forward. Don't let your worries hold you back from pursuing what matters most - taking action and trying new things! Remember: inaction guarantees defeat while perseverance offers hope for success no matter how many setbacks come along the way. So don't give up on yourself or your dreams; instead embrace each challenge as an opportunity to grow stronger and more resilient than ever before!

The fear of what others might say can be overwhelming when considering taking risks or making changes in life. It's true that some people may mock those who choose not to settle for mediocrity; however, these individuals lack the courage necessary for growth and innovation. Those who have never made mistakes likely haven't attempted anything new either! The only way around criticism is by doing nothing at all - saying nothing worthwhile about oneself while living an unremarkable existence devoid of purpose or meaning. This path ultimately leads nowhere fast! Instead embrace change with open arms knowing full well that progress comes from risk-taking and pushing past self-imposed limitations despite any potential ridicule along the journey towards personal fulfillment. You may feel regretful for not starting earlier but don't let that discourage you from taking action now. Remember - it's never too late to begin pursuing your goals! And even if you are older than most people who start on this journey- there is still plenty of time left in life ahead of us all! So why waste it by avoiding something because we think it will take a long time? Time marches forward regardless so might as well use every moment wisely towards our desired outcomes!

It's easy to get discouraged when we think about all the time that has passed since our goals first formed in our minds. But it's important not to dwell on what could have been and instead focus on taking action now! Remember: It's never too late to become who you were meant to be - so start today! Many individuals fail to pursue their dreams due to an overwhelming fear of failure. This is a regrettable reality that must be addressed if we are ever going to achieve true happiness and fulfillment in life. Don't let your fear hold you back from living the life you deserve!

Why do so few people pursue their dreams? According to Les Brown it's because they are living in fear instead. We can no longer allow this paralyzing emotion control our lives; we must find a way forward towards fulfillment of what truly matters most - our aspirations! If not, then we risk wasting precious time working for someone else who benefits from building upon their own goals while neglecting our own desires altogether. Don't let your potential go unrealized – take action today and start making progress towards realizing all that you were meant to be!

It's not necessary to be a genius or experience instant success for us to achieve our goals. The key is perseverance - sticking with it no matter how long it takes or how slowly we progress along the way without giving up hope. If we keep moving forward towards what matters most, anything is possible!

To continue making progress we must find the drive to persist through setbacks without losing our zeal. It's essential that we keep pushing ourselves forward from one failure to another with unwavering enthusiasm. The more we persist, the greater our character becomes. This is something that remains with us forever and ever. It's a true testament to who we are as individuals. So, keep pushing through those challenges - they only make you stronger!

If we want to achieve our dream life goals then it's crucial that we stand tall and confront challenges head on. with courageous determination.

By actively participating in activities which interest us most, we can gain valuable knowledge while also growing as individuals over time - but this alone won't suffice for true transformation; rather than simply changing what we do every day or weekend, its essential that we strive towards becoming different people altogether! This requires a willingness to embrace new experiences outside of comfort zones so that we may evolve into more capable versions of ourselves who are . better equipped handle whatever comes next along the journey ahead.

A pathway towards fulfillment lies within each one of us- all it takes is some gritty determination coupled with an open mindset geared towards constant learning & growth! So go forth bravely today: take risks, try something new, and watch yourself transform before your very eyes...

The world around us is constantly evolving - it's a natural part of life. As humans we too must embrace this change and strive for continual growth if we want to thrive in an ever-changing environment.

To achieve true success both personally & professionally requires that we take on the challenge of becoming better versions of ourselves every day through learning experiences from our surroundings. This approach has been reinforced by my mentor who taught me early on about "being all you can be" as an individual while also contributing positively towards society's well-being. The only way forward? Living life fully!

We are tasked with living our lives to the fullest and should not fret over perfection. The key is putting forth effort towards this goal rather than focusing solely on outcomes. Remember that it's about taking action rather than worrying about results. This mindset will help you achieve greater success in all areas of life! We cannot

FIGHT FOR THE LIFE YOU WANT

control everything that happens around us or the actions of others but we can take charge over our own efforts. By doing so with utmost sincerity and dedication towards achieving success in life - regardless of what it may entail- is all anyone needs to do.

Remember: "The only way forward is through" (John F Kennedy). With this mindset, you'll be able to navigate any obstacle along your journey while always striving for excellence. So, start now by taking actionable steps towards realizing your goals; once achieved they will lead onto even greater opportunities than initially imagined!

May God bless you on this exciting adventure filled with endless possibilities – go forth fearlessly knowing that every step taken brings you closer to where you want to be!

WHERE IS MY WHY?

Made in the USA
Columbia, SC
18 July 2024

38867448R00100